Chapter One

Other books by Jennifer Bacia

Shadows of Power

Angel of Honour

Whisper from the Gods

Mask of Paradise

A Moment in Time

Best Kept Secrets

Creating Popular Fiction

Chapter One

Everything you want to know about starting your novel!

JENNIFER BACIA

ALLEN & UNWIN

First published in 1998 by
Allen & Unwin
9 Atchison Street
St Leonards NSW 2065
Australia

Phone: (61 2) 9901 4088
Fax: (61 2) 9906 2218
E-mail: frontdesk@allen-unwin.com.au
Web: http://www.allen-unwin.com.au

National Library of Australia
Cataloguing-in-Publication entry:

Bacia, Jennifer.
Chapter one: everything you want to know about starting your novel.

ISBN 1 86448 331 8.

1. Fiction—Authorship. 2. Fiction—Technique.
3. Creative writing. I. Title.

808.3

Set in 12/15 pt Bembo by Bookhouse Digital, Sydney
Printed by Australian Print Group, Maryborough, Victoria.

10 9 8 7 6 5 4 3 2 1

Contents

With love for Jean
who gave me the best
gift of all

Introduction

You are not alone.

You've got a great idea for a novel. You've spent weeks, months or even years piecing together some wonderful characters, working out the plotline, deciding on settings. The trouble is, every time you actually sit down and start to write, you seem to freeze. How do you grab the reader's attention right away? How do you transmit all the masses of information you need the reader to know before the story can begin? How do you decide where to start your story?

You type a couple of paragraphs, maybe even a whole page or two. You repeat all that in a dozen different ways, never quite satisfied with what you've put down, before finally tossing away the lot in disgust. It all just seems too hard. You throw up your hands in defeat—and go back to dreaming about the novel you're still determined to write one day.

If the above describes you, then let me repeat: *you are not alone.*

Even people who have been writing professionally for years, who have had dozens of books published, find it difficult, scary even, to face the blank opening pages of their next novel.

So why is starting out so difficult? Why does it seem such a monumental task to get that opening chapter down on paper?

The answer lies mainly in the fact that it is in those first few pages that all the hard work needs to be done. In that brief space you have to introduce and describe your characters and principal setting, place the story in its time frame, choose the point of the plot at which you're going to begin, give readers all the other information they need to know, and raise intriguing questions that will grab their attention immediately.

This tortuous process is known as the *exposition.* It's a demanding task, but if you can pull it off your novel should begin as smoothly as if you wrote it sitting poolside in the Bahamas sipping on a piña colada, or accelerating from zero to 80 kph in a Ferrari.

To achieve such compelling ease of style in those beginning pages is probably the most difficult part of the whole process of writing. Yet I can promise you one thing—if you can manage that, you will have surmounted one of the biggest hurdles in the obstacle race that is completing a novel.

Treat this book as your coach—and your collaborator. Its aim is not only to help you on your way by pointing out the course but to take that first hurdle with you.

Part I offers some insights into the beginnings of my novels, *Shadows of Power, Angel of Honour, Whisper from the Gods, Mask of Paradise, A Moment in Time* and *Best Kept Secrets.* You'll see where I get my ideas from and how I work with them to achieve the story I want to tell. It's certainly not always an easy process but it is extremely rewarding.

In Part 2 you will find many different examples of how to begin a story. Each example will be dissected and analysed to show you exactly how characters can be introduced and described as tellingly as possible, how relevant plot information can be slipped into the exposition in an interesting way, how intrigue can be established right from the start so that readers find they just *have* to keep on reading.

If you like, you may take any of the examples and use it as a starting point for a story of your own. Let it set your imagination running. Ask yourself what might happen next, and how one of them could lead in to your own exciting story. By using it to get you going, you'll also be able to bypass a lot of the hard work of exposition!

In Part 3, I have included a completed short story that I hope will give you further insight into how to move past the beginning to form the middle and the end of a story.

As *The Gift* was published in the *Women's Weekly* as well as in an anthology of short stories, I own the copyright. However, all the opening chapters offered in Part 2 of this book are free of copyright and you may use any of them in the formation of your own novel.

A little bit more about beginning

In my earlier book, *Creating Popular Fiction,* I handle the topic of exposition in detail, but suffice it to say here that the basic information readers need to understand and believe the story is best conveyed as part of the narrative.

Look at this example, for instance: Diana had green eyes and dark curly hair.

Now this: Diana's green eyes were dull with grief as she tied a scarf around her dark, curly hair.

Do you see the difference? In the first example we are merely 'telling' readers something, while in the second we are 'showing', combining the physical description with important information about the character's emotional state. As you read through the sample Chapter Ones presented here, pay close attention to how this interweaving is achieved.

The difficulty with exposition is that it must be handled without losing reader interest. In the opening chapter you have to introduce the main character (almost always), state the conflict or problem she is facing, and establish location and time. The way you tackle this can make the difference between the reader going on avidly or throwing the book out the window.

But at the same time as you convey all this information—and preferably before—you must begin to unfold your plot. Choosing where and how to do this is as important as passing on the necessary background detail. Bear in mind that readers of mass market fiction usually prefer stories that launch them right into the action and raise questions immediately. For this reason it is essential to get the plot up and running before loading them with too much information. Readers need to be made curious before they're interested in a lot of detail about a character. If you begin by merely describing Diana's features, her job and her home and so on, you're going to bore them at once. Why? Because your readers don't care enough yet about Diana to be bothered absorbing all that information.

But what if you start by showing Diana haggard and terrified, on death row? You can bet your bottom dollar that from that point on you'll have your readers hungry for every detail you care to dole out to them. They'll be itching with curiosity to know how Diana could have ended up in such a horrific predicament.

When you're trying to decide where to begin, then, it's always preferable to choose some dramatic moment in your heroine's life rather than launch into a long passage of description or analysis.

That dramatic moment may be told at its proper point in your plot or be related in flashback. This very effective device entails conjuring up an intriguing incident from your character's past and then continuing the story in the present. Let's use Diana again as our example. Perhaps she witnessed a murder when she was a teenager, but has since pushed the traumatic memory out of her mind. We start with that dramatic murder scene and then jump to ten years later, when Diana is working as an assistant to an aspiring politician. The story might deal with the gradual return of her memory and the realisation that the man she works for is in fact the murderer.

It works the opposite way, too. You can open with a flash forward to some crucial point in your heroine's story and then go back and fill in the details of her life up to that point. This time, let's have Diana as an Oscar-winning actress who is in hospital fighting for her life after a murder attempt. Having grabbed the reader's attention with that scene we go back into her past and set out the struggle of her early career. Gradually, as we learn about the enemies she's made on the way to the top, we begin to wonder which of them had the motive and means to kill her.

Another very important point to establish right at the beginning of your story is viewpoint. This is just a technical term for letting readers know through whose eyes the story is being told. Let's go back to our second example and take it a little further: 'Diana's eyes were dull with grief as she tied the scarf around her curly, dark hair. Even now, 48 hours later, she found it impossible to accept the news. She could still remember how cheerful Simon had been that morning when he'd left. He'd been excited, she knew, about the meeting with Harry. "Put the champagne on ice, darling. It's in the bag, I'm sure of it." '

These are Diana's thoughts. Only she knows how Simon was that morning and what he said to her, so although the story is being told in the third person, our viewpoint is through her eyes. Remember, though, that if you use Diana's viewpoint in the first three chapters it will only confuse readers if, in Chapter 4, you change to Susie's viewpoint. It is possible to tell a story effectively from multiple viewpoints, but if this technique is to be used it must be signalled to readers early on.

Viewpoint, and how to handle it, is one of the most difficult hurdles for beginning writers. In *Creating Popular Fiction*, I further explore its mysteries as well as looking more closely at the do's and don'ts of exposition.

Part 1

Starting out

AUTHORS are always being asked where they get their ideas. Well, it's one thing to get an idea for a story. The really hard part is working on that idea to see if it provides enough substance to shape into a full-length plotline.

With this in mind, I thought it might be of benefit here if I tried to explain the germination and development of my own fiction. I have written six novels. *Shadows of Power* was the first to be published, but before that, I had written a 450-page novel, the manuscript of which was contracted by a leading New York literary agency. As things turned out, that manuscript was never published, but I have never looked at the time I spent on it as wasted.

I consider that in that first long work, I served my apprenticeship to the craft of writing. In struggling with the problems that beset me in completing it, I learned invaluable lessons about technique and about the need for discipline and routine. But I also discovered the joys of the creative process. On top of that, I came so close to being published that I knew it would be simply defeatist to allow my initial disappointment to stop me from continuing to write.

Soon afterwards I found a Sydney agent who was actively looking for popular fiction writers. Happily, she confirmed my belief that I had the ability to tell a good tale. Encouraged by her support, I began work on the novel that was to become *Shadows of Power.* My first published novel ended up as a lead title for the publisher in the UK and Australia. It was named a Doubleday Book Club Book of the Month, condensed in *Cosmopolitan,* sold to leading foreign publishers, and snapped up by a major television production company. You'll understand why I'm so glad now that I didn't give up at that first hurdle. My hope is that by retelling my experience I'll have encouraged you not to give up too easily, either.

For me, the idea of writing a novel seems always to have been somewhere in my thoughts. For years, though, it remained vague and half-formed. It wasn't until I started to travel the world that I actually became determined to put my idea into practice.

I remember the time when I lived in Rome as especially influential in this regard. Maybe it was the effect on my senses of all that history and culture. Maybe it was the fact that I had more time than usual on my hands. Then again, it might have had something to do with the fact that one evening I had dinner in the Hotel Nationale, where Scott and Zelda Fitzgerald had once stayed!

I was an incurable romantic about writing and writers—and still am. In the Lake District my thoughts were of Wordsworth; in Oxford I sought out the pub where Thomas Hardy had sat in a corner scribbling parts of *Jude the Obscure*; in Paris I imagined Hemingway's dominating presence. Gradually the urge to try to do what had been in my mind for so long took root and began to grow.

Books had always played a dominant role in my life. I loved reading, and devoured all sorts of novels, across all genres. I have read that many people who have made careers as writers are dedicated diary keepers. This is certainly true in my case. I was also a top English student and was invariably more lucid on paper than with the spoken word.

From an early age I enjoyed the challenge of finding exactly the right words to paint the vivid pictures that I could see in my imagination. I can still remember the mixture of shyness and pride I felt when my eighth-grade teacher read out one of my stories to the class. I was not even fazed when she made the gentle suggestion that in future I might like to limit my efforts to the required two pages instead of 32! I wish I could tell her that I did finally master the short story form too.

The crucial spur to my writing ambitions

occurred in the late 1980s, when novels such as Jackie Collins' *Hollywood Wives*, Shirley Conran's *Lace*, and Sally Beauman's *Destiny* were being published amid loud fanfare. Along with millions of other women I read these books for pleasure, but I also found myself beginning to analyse them in an attempt to figure out how their authors had created such successes. Slowly, hardly even realising it at first, I was getting ready to take the plunge.

Shadows of Power

As I make clear in *Creating Popular Fiction*, there are fashions in fiction just as in most other aspects of culture. If you do as I did, you'll begin not by typing, but by studying the market to figure out what is selling! That way you will give yourself a much better chance of being published.

When I began what was to become my full-time writing career, blockbuster best-sellers were very much in vogue. So I set out to produce the sort of story that would meet the characteristics of that genre—larger-than-life characters, exotic locations and a plot filled with action and drama.

Authors are often asked which they think up first: characters or plot? In *Shadows of Power*, it was the character of Anthea James who first fired my imagination. I wanted to create a heroine who was strong, resourceful and driven. Someone other women looked up to. A woman making her mark in a man's world, who could achieve her goals on her own terms—but without sacrificing her femininity. Virtually all my heroines have been suggested by real-life women, and in this case it was publisher Ita Buttrose—a high-profile media personality, Businesswoman of the Year, one of Australia's most admired women—who provided the initial spark for Anthea. I've never met Ita, and that's probably a good thing, as I would never model a character too closely on a living person. It was merely Ita's image that inspired me. From there I created the imaginary character I needed to tell my story.

While keeping in mind the sorts of heroines other successful authors were creating, I also wanted Anthea James to be different. To this end I made her a little older than the norm and gave her a rather different background from the then-usual Rodeo Drive, ritzy department stores, and five-star international hotels. Spurred by my interest in politics, I decided to create a heroine whose driving ambition was to be the first female prime minister of Australia.

One of the first questions I had to ask myself, though, was what reason she could have for desiring this goal so badly. It couldn't be merely for the trappings of power; readers would find little to identify with in such a self-seeking character. As strong motivation is one of the essentials of good plotting, I had to come up with a more meaningful underpinning for my heroine's ambition.

While I was mulling over this problem the answer came to me in the easiest of ways. I picked up the newspaper one weekend and read an investigative report on Asian women who were being lured to Australia and forced into prostitution. At once I knew I had it! Anthea, I decided, would be raised by the madam of Sydney's most infamous brothel. She would see at first hand what happened to women who lacked valid options and opportunities. And that experience would give her the drive and determination to do all she could to help women achieve financial equality. (What is interesting about this part of the storyline is that although *Shadows of Power* was written in 1987, the subject of Asian prostitution is still as topical as ever more than ten years later.)

Having sorted out my main character's motivation, I now had to decide what form of opposition she would face as she pursued her goal. I had to devise a character or characters who would be hell bent on destroying Anthea's carefully laid plans.

It didn't take me very long to come up with a villain in the guise of Anthea's employer, the media mogul Julian Crane. Keeping these two characters interacting in the workplace—Anthea was a media star—made for plenty of conflict and pointed the way to another essential of the blockbuster: the subplot.

Shadows of Power had numerous subplots. One involved Anthea's problems with Crane as she sought to pursue a story to which he strenuously objected. Another involved Anthea's romantic interest. Yet another involved a third party to that romantic interest. There were quite a few others, too, but each was essential to the story, not merely padding. I discuss the full structure of *Shadows of Power* in much broader detail in *Creating Popular Fiction.*

As my plot began to take shape in my mind, I realised I would have to start my story with a device common to a lot of suspense fiction: a prologue, which would launch my readers into the story at a point of high tension and grab their attention immediately.

After I completed the manuscript, I must have gone back and written those opening pages at least three dozen times. Even now I can see ways to improve them. I say this to remind you that the important thing when you start writing is not to let yourself get bogged down in trying to write the perfect beginning. Just get the book started. You can always come back and rewrite the opening afterwards. Getting the story rolling will also give you a stronger sense of your characters and build your confidence by showing you a slowly growing pile of finished pages.

Here is how *Shadows of Power* began:

From the doorway the girl stared boldly at the man who sat naked on the blue silk cover of the bed.

She could handle this one. She knew his tastes were...exotic, but she wasn't afraid. And she had been assured that her co-operation would be amply rewarded.

In silence, the man watched the girl enter the dimly lit room. Her unclothed body was perfect. She was about nineteen with full, firm breasts and long, strong legs. As she came closer he could smell the musky perfume of her body, the scent of her flowing fair hair.

His cold, blue eyes travelled slowly over her. Her beauty had no effect. His penis lay slack and indifferent between his pale spreading thighs.

Still without speaking he indicated that she join him on the bed. The girl moved to obey and lay next to but not touching him, her heavily made-up eyes holding his.

The man stared down into the soft, young face and it was then he felt the first stirring in his loins. He imagined those same eyes stark with

> fear, those full, childlike lips twisted in pain and the thought made him grow firmer.

In this start, neither of the protagonists is named and the viewpoint of each is used. As well, the reader is given enough information to understand very quickly that these are two strangers and the setting is probably a brothel. The girl already knows that the man's tastes are 'exotic', so it can be assumed that he has visited the brothel on previous occasions. The passage also implies that he enjoys kinky sex for which the girl knows she will be 'amply rewarded'.

Then we get some insight into the man. We learn that the young girl's beauty has no effect on him. What does turn him on is the thought of those youthful eyes 'stark with fear', those 'lips twisted in pain'.

By the end of this short opening scene, readers shouldn't be surprised to learn that the girl is murdered by her client.

Once that is divulged, the questions begging to be answered are: who is the man and why is he driven to kill? How will he be linked to the heroine? Will he kill anyone else?

The scene captures readers' attention in a dramatic way and keeps them turning the pages.

Angel of Honour

Although the plotline for my first novel fell quickly into place, I had a much more difficult time with *Angel of Honour.* Part of the problem was the increased pressure I was under. Having achieved such heady success with *Shadows of Power,* I knew I had to produce at least as good a story again—hopefully, an even better one. Over a period of almost fifteen months I tried out dozens of different storylines, but none of them came to life enough to inspire me to keep writing. My major means of detecting when a story isn't working is my own sense of boredom with it. If I'm bored I know for certain my readers will be too.

What I needed to find again was that same sense of excitement about an idea that I had had with *Shadows of Power.* None of the heroines I was creating managed to catch my imagination as Anthea James had done.

Then, one evening, as I was watching the evening news, I saw the crowds in Nicaragua milling around their new president, Violeta Chamorro. Chamorro was a 50-year-old ex-newspaper magnate, a woman who had changed career in midstream for the good of her country.

Surely not the stuff of popular-fiction heroines, I can hear you thinking. But for me that news item generated the idea of a woman untrained, unprepared for public office, someone who, for love of her country, had to turn her back on the world she had known to that point. And the real-life person who at once sprang to my mind was Princess Stephanie of Monaco.

I immediately began asking myself the 'what ifs'.

What if the young and glamorous Stephanie had suddenly found herself in the same position? What if the playgirl rebel had been forced to change her ways and take on the heavy mantle of political responsibility?

Keep in mind that one of the essentials of good plotting is to have the main character grow and change as the story develops. In *Shadows of Power* I had the naive young Anthea, a 'good girl', shocked into the awareness that led to her drive to fight for women's rights.

In this new story I would have a 'bad girl' heroine, a wilful, spoilt young woman, interested only in the superficial, forced to change her life when she was handed the reins of her family's political dynasty.

Once again I had based a character on a real woman—or in this case women—and had chosen a political theme to add suspense and intrigue to the rich love story.

The setting, I decided, would be a fictitious South American country; an amalgam of Costa Rica,

Nicaragua and Argentina, and I spent a lot of time researching the histories, politics and problems of these countries. However, I had to keep in mind that although I am interested in world politics, a lot of my readers wouldn't necessarily be so enthralled. So I laced this information gently through the story—never inserting too much, just enough to add interest and credibility.

My next problem was to decide on the conflict in the story.

Noella de Bartez, my heroine, is first portrayed as shallow and self-interested, so the earliest source of conflict in the story is with her father. Vincent de Bartez, the recently elected President of Martiguay, is trying to restore the country to democracy after years of military rule. He is a widower whose wife has died in an accident for which Noella guiltily feels responsible. By adding this psychological dimension to Noella's character I provide a possible excuse for her childhood rebelliousness and so keep her sympathetic to my readers.

I also decided to give Noella an elder sister who would provide a contrast to her. Gabrielle is the 'good daughter', who is as much a patriot as her father. Noella, on the other hand, hasn't the slightest interest in politics. Her only desire is to get away from Martiguay and the stifling confines of her family and palace protocol.

Of course the only means of escape for a girl of her upbringing is marriage—which gave me the opportunity to introduce a playboy type who plays a vital role in the plot.

By the second half of the book, Noella has a different motivation as she fights to save her country from a despotic military junta backed by the drug lords. This offers the opportunity to show her transformation from a spoilt young woman to an inspiring leader battling the forces of evil.

As in *Shadows of Power*, subplots play an important part in this story. One involves Noella's disastrous marriage, another deals with the man she loves but cannot have because of her commitment to her country. Yet another involves her ongoing relationship with Paolo, the poor stable boy who was her first lover. I must say here that when I wrote the early lovemaking scene between Paola and Noella, who seduces him on her sister's wedding day, my aim was merely to show my heroine's rebellious nature. Only as the story progressed did I realise what a strong and useful character Paolo could be if I brought him back into Noella's life at a later date.

In *Angel of Honour* I used many more secondary characters than in *Shadows of Power*. If you take note as you read the novel, you will see that each is there for a specific purpose. All have a role to fulfil. Secondary characters should never be mere padding.

CHAPTER ONE

Again I began with a prologue. I did not actually write this, though, until I was almost halfway through the story. By then I knew what high point of the plot would best work for the opening.

This is how I began:

The killer was in no hurry. He knew his victim's schedule and the Citroën was parked just minutes away. He had plenty of time.

As he sipped at his expresso he watched the passersby on the Rue de Rivoli. It was the end of September and the tourist barbarians were almost gone. Once more the city belonged to the Parisians.

It was surprisingly warm and the man sweated in his English tailored suit. His stylish clothes gave little clue to his nationality: Lanvin shirt, silk tie from de Casi New York, French calfskin shoes from Lobbs of St James. Long ago the killer had recognised the universal human failing which allowed a man to be judged by his dress. At all levels officialdom was more easily deflected by the appearance of distinction and elegance. Neither the firm from which he'd hired the Citroën nor French Customs nor police had presented him with any problem.

Not that he'd expected any. The assignment

> was simple enough, the victim's schedule as predictable as the Swiss.

Again, I begin with an unnamed character, one who is immediately identified as a killer. And not just any thug: this man, it is implied, is a professional. Therefore, it might be assumed, his target is someone important. The whole idea of such a meticulously planned exercise adds to the sense of menace and intrigue and immediately raises the questions: who is to be killed and why? As the prologue continues, readers learn that the killer's intended victim is the heroine of the story.

Whisper from the Gods

The germ of this book lay in my fascination with the tragic legend of the Kennedys. No writer could ever have imagined the incredible true-life tale of this American political dynasty. I was particularly fascinated by JFK's charismatic son, John Jr. I imagined the excitement it would have caused in Democratic Party ranks if the late president's heir had chosen a political career.

This idea strongly appealed to me as the basis for a story, but I knew the character I would base on John Jr couldn't be the main character of my story.

I had to keep pondering the problem of how to come up with a plausible heroine.

Of course the Marilyn Monroe story wasn't too far out of my mind, either, and it was in pursuing that line that I finally brought my heroine to life.

This time the 'what ifs' went something like this:

What if an ambitious young woman became head of a major, yet ailing, film studio? What if she was planning to make a movie that purported to tell the true story about how the actress I call Elizabeth Eden died? What if this sent shivers through the ranks of those campaigning to get the late President's son, Robbie Madigan, elected to the White House?

This scenario not only gave me an interesting heroine with a strong motivation (you'll understand how strong if you have read the novel!) but also powerful forces opposed to her.

As well, I worked out subplots involving various people with very strong reasons for wishing to prevent the movie on Elizabeth Eden from being made.

To further enrich the story I decided to make Robbie Madigan a reluctant contender for the office of President. This was something I imagined might easily have been the case with John Kennedy Jr, who, burdened by his name and heritage, could have felt pressured into running for office by his late father's close aides and supporters.

In my story I also decided to make Robbie

Madigan's mother obsessively intent on seeing another Madigan in the White House. Although in real life I feel fairly certain that Jackie Kennedy would have had no desire to relive those days through her son, Estelle Madigan is determined to enjoy vicariously the power and privilege that was snatched so cruelly from her all those years ago.

Once again, I aimed to grab my readers' attention with an opening that set up a mystery:

> He called it the Shrine.
>
> It was his secret place. His place of worship. A sanctum where the dream lived on and his fantasies could still come true.
>
> Face flushed with anticipation, the Idolator allowed his eyes to travel slowly over the walls. Her photograph was everywhere, covering every inch of space. He knew that with a flick of a switch he could hear her voice, the voice that never failed to thrill him.
>
> He made his selection from the stack of videos as he had done so often before. He placed the cassette in the machine, then crossed to a small, locked cabinet in the corner of the room. With reverent care he removed a slim, cardboard box embossed with the name of an exclusive store.
>
> Breath quickening, the Idolator switched off the overhead light and settled himself in the

comfortable low-backed chair. He was ready. Ready for an experience he knew would be almost spiritual in its intensity.

Again, I have broken one of the unwritten 'rules' of popular fiction, which states that the main character should be introduced as quickly as possible. But, as in *Shadows of Power,* this prologue is short and full of intrigue. It doesn't delay the introduction of the heroine too long while setting the tone of the story.

It's pretty clear in this beginning that we're dealing with a man with an obsession. The room he calls the Shrine is dedicated to the object of his desire. By the end of the prologue readers should want to know who the Idolator is and who he is obsessed with. Having been drawn in, they'll now be prepared to absorb the exposition that will be essential to establish the heroine and her motivation.

Mask of Paradise

Mask of Paradise grew out of a desire to explore a part of my own heritage. I have very vivid memories of my first visit to Poland as a teenager. Then, the Communists were still in power and the country was under military rule. Armed soldiers patrolled the streets, buildings still showed the scars of the Second World War, and there wasn't a can of Coca-Cola in sight! Yet for all the sense of deprivation, it was in Warsaw that I attended my first opera, ballet, and symphony concert. This initial journey to my late father's homeland made a very deep impression, so much so that I have visited half a dozen times since.

It was only natural, therefore, that I should be drawn to this locale as the background for a novel—especially as, around the time I was starting my third book, the Iron Curtain was coming down in Eastern Europe. It seemed a wonderful scenario in which to set a story, and I even planned a trip to Moscow to get a first-hand sense of the historic events.

Yet despite my enthusiasm, the usual frustrations faced me. Every time I came up with what I thought was a strong and interesting character and some intriguing plot twists, I ran into a problem: what was my heroine's motivation? What was she driven by? Who or what was trying to stop her?

At first I envisaged my main character as a woman in her 70s. Through flashbacks to her girlhood in Poland, I would trace her life story and her success when she emigrated to Australia after the war.

But try as I might, I couldn't get the various angles I was playing with to work. I had a wonderful background figured out, had even written the first 30 pages of my account of my heroine's childhood, but I still couldn't decide exactly where I was heading. What was my heroine's ultimate goal? And why was she so driven to achieve it?

My frustration was all the greater because this was a subject I passionately wanted to write about. But the key I needed to open the story continued to elude me.

Again, it was through watching television that the answer eventually came to me—which is why I am an avid viewer of news and current affairs programs! On this occasion the show dealt with television personality Jana Wendt's trip to Czechoslovakia to search for the files kept on her father by the former Communist government. As I watched Jana walking between the rows of grey files, I knew with a shiver of excitement that I had found my heroine. This time she was a young Australian woman, the daughter of a Polish mother who had come to Australia as a wartime refugee and married into a wealthy Sydney family.

When the ball finally starts rolling for me, it rolls hard and fast. I could barely scribble down my ideas quickly enough now that I had at last broken the impasse. It was suddenly clear to me that I would tell two stories in this novel: the mother's story and the daughter's. The first would begin in pre-war Europe, the other in present-day Australia.

At this stage, too, I decided the tale should begin with the daughter, a high-profile current affairs show presenter, facing a murder charge. Who she'd killed, or why, I had not the slightest idea! But that didn't worry me. I have always trusted my abilities enough to know that I will find a way around most problems as long as I've solved the main ones: my heroine's motivation and the story's source of conflict. In the end, it wasn't until I was almost halfway through the manuscript that I finally decided on the person she stood accused of murdering!

I did know early on, however, that my heroine, Eve Taylor, was driven by an obsessive need to discover the secret of her mother's past. Why had her mother, Marianne, spent 20 years in a Sydney mental institution? What terrible event had robbed her of her memory and speech? As Eve sought to unravel the mystery, she would be opposed in her quest by her late father's family.

When her husband died prematurely, Marianne had found herself at the mercy of her wealthy but vicious mother-in-law, Edwina, who firmly believed that her son had been tricked into marriage by this worthless Polish refugee and was determined to wreak a terrible revenge.

There are fewer subplots in this novel than in my earlier works, probably because there are really two parallel main plots.

Here's how *Mask of Paradise* began:

CHAPTER ONE

It was the soft yielding of female flesh that turned Harry Bowman on. His hands stroked the silky softness of thighs, hips, breasts, and excitement surged within him. Now, with a groan he lowered his head and burrowed his face between the pale moons of breasts that never failed to arouse him.

Not even now. At close to sixty-three years of age.

But the woman lying beneath him did more than arouse his lusts. She had brought him back to life.

That was the way Harry saw it anyway.

He knew there were plenty among his colleagues who had laughed behind his back when they found out he'd asked Margaret to marry him. That was almost two years ago and she'd just turned thirty-two.

Jealous of course, he'd told himself. Because he'd managed to land himself a young woman. But then he hadn't let himself go like the rest of them. He was too vain for that. Even in Sydney he'd swum daily, played tennis at his club and kept himself fit. He was proud too of his head of thick if greying hair.

But more than twenty years at the Bar hadn't left Harry Bowman with too many illusions. As one of the country's leading criminal lawyers his fees matched his legendary reputation and he was now a very rich man.

He felt certain that in all probability it was his wealth rather than his sharp and seasoned mind or his reputation and acclaim that had been the motivation to marriage for the slim, curly-haired brunette who now moaned beneath him.

Yet Harry Bowman had been a pragmatist—and a widower—too long to worry overly about that. He loved showing off his young, pretty wife, loved having someone to spoil and indulge, and if his happiness lasted just a short time, well he would accept it on those terms.

It had taken a heart attack six months before to convince the high-flying lawyer he had married a woman who genuinely loved him.

With compassion and patience Margaret had nursed him back to health. And then it was she who had insisted that they get out of Sydney, away from the rat race he'd endured for so long.

'Let's be totally unoriginal, darling,' she'd said one night when they were discussing the future. 'What about going north? Sunshine, warmth, minimum stress. What do you think?'

She was stroking his scrotum during their first sexual exchange since his attack and Harry felt filled with the heat of passion and conviction.

The transition had been unbelievably easy.

Within weeks they were ensconced in a double storey beachside mansion decorated in the colours of the sea and sky and Harry felt as if God had shown him the path to heaven.

Life was as good as it was ever going to get, he thought now, as he dug his fingers into his wife's grinding buttocks. Margaret, the house, the environment, and just the odd interesting case to keep his brain ticking over.

He could feel his climax approaching. Margaret's quivering breathing told him she was right there with him. An experienced lover, Harry knew better than to spoil her intense concentration with too frenzied movements. Together, slowly, they climbed the path to dark, unconscious bliss.

And then the abruptness of the interruption killed it for both of them. His wife slumped back from his embrace and swore ferociously under her breath.

'What the hell...' Harry glanced at the bedside alarm as the telephone shrilled in the darkness. Five after ten. When he'd been at the peak of his profession, late night calls invariably meant trouble.

'Shall I answer it?' His wife's voice revealed her annoyance.

'No, leave it to the machine.' Harry felt his erection die. 'Probably a wrong bloody number.'

But Harry Bowman was mistaken. As the answering machine clicked on, he heard a voice he recognised and a message that brought him instantly alert.

Beside him, his wife held her breath and listened too.

'...it's urgent Harry. You're the only one I can trust. They're charging her with murder.'

With a rush of the old, familiar adrenalin Harry Bowman knew it was going to be a long night.

Australia woke to the scandal the following morning. The story was headline news around the nation. Shock and disbelief were the almost universal reaction.

Eve Taylor.

A devastating combination of brains and beauty. At thirty-three, Australia's top-rating media personality.

A woman who had interviewed presidents and kings, whose ruthless pursuit of the facts invoked fear among prime ministers and corporate fat cats alike. For three years her prime-time program, *Taylor Made*, had operated at the nation's cutting edge, dominating the ratings as it broke major story after story.

> And now, in an almost cannibalistic orgy, it was Eve Taylor herself who was being devoured by the media machine she had ruled over for so long.

Unblushingly, I start once more with a sex scene. But this is one that offers a lot more than physical mechanics. What I've done here is draw a detailed background for Harry Bowman that establishes him more intimately with the reader. It serves in a way as the 'lull before the storm'. I'm hoping that before they even realise it, readers will be drawn into the relationship between Harry Bowman, successful barrister, and his young wife, and will, step by step, be drawn towards the moment when the phone rings and Harry hears something that gives him the 'old, familiar rush of adrenalin'.

And I immediately explain why. Because Australia's top-rating current affairs anchor has been charged with murder.

The prologue ends with a short scene that also introduces the other protagonist, Eve's mother, Marianne. Incapable of speech, she is sitting in the garden of her cottage in the Blue Mountains being cared for by an old friend who wonders in despair if the mother's curse has now been extended to the next generation.

By now my readers should be well and truly hooked.

A Moment in Time

All of my first four novels had been optioned for film and television rights, but as their plot complexities meant they were only translatable into expensive mini-series, their progress towards production was repeatedly stymied. For that reason, I determined to come up with a concept for a novel that could be transferred reasonably easily to the medium of film. I hoped that once one book was taken on by Hollywood, the ball would start rolling for all the others!

The plot for *A Moment in Time* was the only one that has ever come to me as a completed concept in a single day. This was a miracle I don't expect to happen again, but for all that, it didn't happen without the usual trial and error process—months of effort trying out a myriad of other ideas. Still, when the idea finally came, it did so all at once. The leading characters were instantly real to me, and the theme interested me enormously.

It came about like this: I was taking my dog on her usual daily walk when I passed the farmer who owned the land through which I was walking. He was astride his tractor, a tall, good-looking man in his 60s. As always, he raised his hat and called out a greeting when he saw me.

I suspected he was a widower, as I had never seen a wife, and it was at that instant that the idea for my story fell out of the heavens. In my excitement I could hardly wait to get back home and start making notes.

The basic premise of the story rested on the question of why women so often look for a partner among men more upwardly mobile than themselves. Wouldn't they give themselves a much wider choice, I asked myself, if they looked further afield than just professionals? Of course taking that avenue would mean having to deal with their own expectations and prejudices, not to mention those of their friends...

And so the character of Maddy Tyler was born.

A Moment in Time is a very contemporary women's story. On one level it is about the affair between a sophisticated career woman and an easy-going, unworldly farmer, and on other levels it addresses the issues of social expectations, the values of the 90s, and the need for balance in our lives.

I got the momentum for the story from newspaper stories I had read on the growing numbers of single women trawling a supposedly shrinking pool of appropriate partners. This isn't my heroine's problem, though: she has already given up and opted out of the race. Maddy had a short, wonderful marriage which ended in her young husband's death and now, at 42 and with too many affairs behind her, she has finally come to accept that she will never be able to replace him. These days all her energy and passion are focused on the art gallery she runs so successfully.

Maddy is the quintessential chic, sophisticated, inner-city dweller—until she is shocked into re-evaluating her life by a heart attack brought on by the pressures of work. In search of tranquillity, she finds a weekend retreat in the country. And it's then that she meets Fraser O'Neill, the farmer who is her neighbour.

In this story the main conflict derives from within the main character. Maddy is a woman used to being in control. When she begins an affair with Fraser she never suspects that he will take it seriously. After all, they're worlds apart. How could he even dream that she'd want anything more than a fling?

Character development thus becomes a major feature of *A Moment in Time* as Maddy confronts her own hang-ups and prejudices, as well as the more important issues of life and death. Locale is important, too, as the contrast is drawn between city and country life and the differing values of each lifestyle. And the several subplots help to give depth and emotional focus to the main characters.

CHAPTER ONE

As this was the first novel I had written without a strong element of suspense, it was crucial that I find some other way to engage my readers' attention right from the start. Like everything else about this novel, the beginning came to me very easily:

> We have no way of knowing when we wake to the day, the hour, that will change our lives. There is nothing that whispers to us: this is the moment in time. Life has no early warning system.
>
> That morning Madeline Tyler rose taking life on trust as usual. She was an attractive, fair-haired woman of forty-two—though in her mind she still thought of herself as a girl. She was petite, slim, though not firm—at least not by the standards women set for themselves these days. Maddy's idea of fitness had been to give up cigarettes on her twenty-fifth birthday. It was nervous energy and self-discipline that kept her thin. She had a bony, interesting face and grey-blue eyes that had gradually lost their open frankness of twenty years before. These days they were a little dulled by the membrane of caution and disillusion.
>
> Maddy Tyler's forty-two years had not, been without their trials.

It's the intrigue implied in the opening sentence

that should make readers willing to accept the necessarily detailed exposition that follows. What is it that is going to change Maddy Tyler's life? What will be her reaction and how far-reaching the effects? *A Moment in Time* offers a more low-key drama than my other books, but by drawing Maddy as a woman my readers can relate to, I hoped to make them keen to share her 'journey'.

Best Kept Secrets

This novel was also prompted by a desire to explore the dilemmas faced by contemporary women. All around me I was hearing women I know discussing the pros and cons of their careers, their relationships, their children and lifestyles and their efforts to harmonise all these things. These very topical issues were what I wanted to look at in my next novel.

Because there were a number of dilemmas I wished to explore, I decided I would need three main characters to provide the scope and opportunity to contrast different viewpoints and lifestyles. The characters became Cass, Fran and Angela.

I introduced Cass as that rarity—a married woman who has never worked (except at bringing up three children!). For her, the conflict emerged from the fact that her job as a mother was now over and she had nothing of importance to fill the vacuum in her life. Her self-esteem was at an all-time low as she compared herself to the smart, young women who worked alongside her advertising executive husband.

Character development, of course, is essential to any well-told story, and Cass had change forced upon her when her husband left her for a younger woman. As the story progressed, I showed her developing from a weak and dependent woman to one who was in charge of her own life. A second source of conflict was established when she went back to study and became involved with a much younger man. Not only did this relationship cause a dilemma for Cass, but she also had to deal with her teenage daughter's open antagonism to her affair.

In contrast, Fran was a successful litigation lawyer who was still single. Her inner conflict centred on the fact that she actually hated the career that had brought her such material success. What she really wanted was a husband and family. To further complicate matters, I decided to have Fran fall in love with a married man, one who would never leave his wife to care for their intellectually disabled child alone.

My third heroine, Angela, was a career woman proud of her independence and the fact that she needed no man. I established a motivation for her fierce independence and lack of desire for marriage by relating it to an incident from her childhood. When Angela was just seven years old her father had walked out on the family. Seeing her mother's helplessness in the face of such abandonment, she had determined never to allow herself to depend on any male.

Angela lived for her career as a top-rating television presenter and I decided to explore women's fear of aging by showing how, at almost 40, she was threatened by an ambitious younger woman. I based Angela's character development on a totally unforeseeable crisis that would bring her the realisation that human intimacy is not always something to fear.

As always, I tried to develop characters who were facing issues and dilemmas I myself would find interesting to explore. Like *A Moment in Time,* this story also emphasised the value of female friendship. I didn't realise until I'd almost finished doing my notes that it would also contain an element of suspense: by the end of the novel one of the characters would die. And to make sure I kept my readers riveted on the story, I disclosed this fact in the last sentence of Chapter 1!

As in *A Moment in Time,* I wasn't starting with a murder, an assassination attempt or a sex scene. But I still had to make sure I grabbed my readers' interest as soon as possible. So I chose to open the story with a provocative statement and then very quickly make clear that Cass was hiding a secret as she entertained guests at the usual New Year's Eve party at her harbourside home.

Here is how *Best Kept Secrets* began:

She couldn't help wondering why it was love that so often taught the true meaning of hate.

Around midnight, after she'd performed the ritual hugs and kisses and cliched best wishes, the emotion surged through her again, choking off her breath.

But still, Cass congratulated herself bitterly, she was managing the impossible. Keeping her secret to herself. Hiding it behind the forced bonhomie of the moment as she moved around the crowded living room. Johnny's friends mostly. 'Friends' he felt they should know. The city's movers and shakers. The people who knew people who knew people.

She hadn't wanted a party this year. Not after what had happened. But she had known there was little chance of talking Johnny out of something that had become such a fixture on their social calendar. Johnny Dunworth was a party man. Throwing, or going to—Johnny knew how to have a good time. Even at a party for two.

Just these few opening paragraphs make clear that Cass is a woman under pressure, prompting readers to read on to find out why.

In Chapter 1, I also introduced the other two leading characters, both of whom were present at the party:

> Fran Antoni hated New Year. She hated parties also. Parties too obviously revealed her as the freak she felt herself to be. If she'd been divorced she could at least have laid claim to fitting society's norms. But there was nothing normal about being a thirty-nine-year-old never married woman.

> Angela Kelly was worried. Sometimes she wondered if it was the natural state for people employed in her fickle industry. Still, she did her best to comfort herself, she had survived longer than most. Twenty years in the business and now prime time anchor on *Deadline*. The current affairs show everyone watched. Five years she'd lasted. An eternity for anyone, and particularly for a female of the species.

As you will have noted, both the above paragraphs take the reader straight into the characters' heads and to the heart of their dilemmas. Aspects like physical description and backgrounds came come later, *after* you've got your readers hooked.

Juggling more than one main character is obviously a little bit more difficult, but if you decide to do this in your own story bear in mind the importance of introducing all of them as early as possible. That way readers will understand at once that they are about to embark on a multi-viewpoint tale, that is, one told through more than one character's eyes.

By now you will have seen that the work of starting a novel is never easy, even when you're a professional author. It takes persistence and determined effort to develop the many elements that are vital to a good yarn, and to come up with a plotline of substance.

I hope that, as you read the different chapter beginnings that follow in Part 2, you will find the inspiration you need to start your own creative juices flowing.

Part 2

Chapter One

CHAPTER ONE

The headlights of the Daimler cut through the darkness.

He rarely allowed himself the pleasure of taking the wheel himself but tonight, as he left London behind, his thoughts were far from the delights of driving the superbly tuned machine. A pulse drummed agonisingly in his left temple, and his palms were damp around the leather-covered steering wheel.

The traffic on the motorway was light at that time on a Sunday night, and in less than an hour he had arrived at the exit to Bartham.

As he took the Daimler easily around the curves of the narrow country lanes, he recalled the many weekends he'd spent at Bartham Hall in the last eight years. The Georgian house set in 500 rolling acres was where he had so often entertained the elite and powerful, cementing the connections which had allowed his empire to expand and prosper.

CHAPTER ONE

As James Beauman turned off the lane and brought the car to a halt in front of a pair of magnificent scrolled gates, he knew that after what had happened nothing would ever be the same again.

He pushed the electric eye on the dashboard and the gates swung slowly open. He hadn't informed the staff of his arrival, but the red glow of the sensor would alert them to his presence. Normally he was a creature of routine and habit, and they would, no doubt, be surprised by this late and unexpected arrival.

James Beauman's lips twisted in a bitter parody of a smile. Well, there were a few more surprises to come.

As he alighted from the car on the curved pebble driveway, he saw the glow of lights from the staff quarters at the rear. Yet no one would disturb him, he was sure of that.

In the cavernous hallway he snapped on one of the two magnificent chandeliers, then hesitated at the entrance to the sitting room.

Why not? he thought. His courage needed no bolstering—he had made up his mind—yet he saw no reason to deny himself the pleasure of a fine glass of whiskey.

His footsteps made no sound on the thick Axminster and he had just picked up the

Waterford decanter when he was disturbed by the ringing of the telephone.

Damn. His face darkened. Not now. Not this evening.

But it was the internal line, and he heard the soft Scottish burr of Jackson on the other end.

'Wasn't expecting you, sir. Just wondered if you required me.' The respectful, soothing tones of the perfect servant. A man who knew his job was easier than most and was determined to do nothing to lose it.

'No, Jackson. Thank you. Don't disturb yourself.' James was surprised at the steadiness in his voice. And as he replaced the receiver he thought obliquely how faultless Janet had always been in her choice of domestic staff. You concentrate on the business, darling, she would say, leave the rest to me.

And as he filled his glass, bitterness again twisted his lips. In the end, it seemed, his wife had proved better at her job than he at his.

He drank the whisky in one long swallow, and as he placed the empty tumbler back on the silver tray he took a moment to dwell on the beauty of the room—on the elegant mix of antique and traditional furnishings, on the superb marble fireplace that had cost him a small fortune to restore, on the Degas that was now worth almost twenty times what he had paid for it.

Material possessions, James Beauman thought. The measure of success, realised ambition. Yet nothing, he knew now, compared to a man's reputation.

His expression hardening, he turned and hurried from the room, the urgency once more within him.

In the wood-panelled gun room his fingers trembled only slightly as he unlocked the walnut cabinet and lifted the ivory-handled pistol from its padded bed.

It was exactly five minutes after midnight when the single shot broke the chilly silence of the night.

Why it works

Now let's take a closer look and find out what makes this a good opening chapter. We'll examine what information we've given the reader and note the use of mystery and intrigue to ensure a gripping beginning. We'll also look at the various possibilities for continuing the story.

The first paragraph, a single sentence, is deliberately vivid—almost filmic. For me, a suspense story always works best when it jumps straight into the action. And even in this first sentence we provide some clues. The Daimler car suggests someone wealthy; the allusion to darkness adds to the intrigue.

In the next paragraph the character is introduced, but not immediately named. At this early stage of the story we don't want to waste time setting out that sort of detail. Instead we rush our readers into the action—and again suggest that this character is seriously wealthy. 'He rarely allowed himself the pleasure of taking the wheel himself' implies, of course, that he has a chauffeur.

By now, too, we have hinted at the location of the story, not far from London. We have also introduced the first hint of mystery and suspense by describing the man's anxious state. At once readers should be asking themselves why the man's pulse is drumming and why his palms are damp around the wheel. But the way to make suspense writing really work is to postpone answering those questions for as long as possible!

These first three sentences have already done a great deal of work.

In the next couple of paragraphs, we fill in a little more of our character's background. We offer more detail about his home as well as the important fact that he is someone who mixes with 'the elite and powerful'. This again raises the question of what could be so upsetting to a man in his position.

Only in paragraph 5 do we finally give our character a name—a good, solid Anglo-Saxon name which firms up the character's social context. And again we don't let more than a couple of sentences pass without reminding readers that something is amiss: 'he knew that after what had happened nothing would ever be the same again.' Never forget that the secret to suspense writing is to keep the reader guessing, wanting to know why and how.

In paragraph 7 we reinforce the growing suspense by hinting at the sort of trouble facing James Beauman. But again we offer no answers.

The writing in this all-important passage is very visual. We give a strong sense of the opulence of Beauman's home, but without any superfluous descriptions, just enough to paint the scene: a brief mention of the Axminster carpet, the magnificent chandeliers, the Waterford crystal. Too much detail at this point would slow down the story and irritate readers, who by now should be intrigued to know exactly what Beauman's problem is.

To tease them on, we let drop the fact that 'his courage needed no bolstering'. At this stage an astute reader might get her first hint of what is to come...

Then, bang! The telephone rings, and our character's edgy response should further add to the suspense.

When Jackson, Beauman's servant, is introduced,

we give just enough detail to sketch him in clearly: a name, an accent, an attitude. All these things add to the reality of the story. Think how much more blandly it would have read if we'd merely written, 'It was his butler on the line.'

Next we allude to Beauman's wife, so the reader will know our character's a married man—and, tellingly, one who feels his wife is better at her job than he is at his. Now at last, we are giving some answers to the questions we've set up. James Beauman's problems appear to be tied to his business. And paragraph 18 hints that whatever has gone wrong has left some stain on his business reputation—such a bad stain, in fact, that this privileged man can't bear to face the future.

Now the interesting work begins for you. This is where you start asking yourself how you might develop this intriguing opening chapter into a novel.

Here are a few things to think about:

- Is James Beauman going to be your main character? If so, you will now have to use flashback to tell his life story. Let the reader in on his early background, how he made his money, his personal life, his enemies, and what went wrong.
- Don't forget that as the hero, James Beauman must be a 'good guy'. Given that, the predicament he faces at the start of the story must not be his

own fault but has probably been caused by his enemies.

- It is seldom a good idea to have your hero kill himself in Chapter 1. But it could be his close shave with death that makes Beauman decide to take on the impossible odds and fight back to prove his innocence or expose his blackmailers. To add to the suspense, however, we could defer letting readers know that Beauman has survived until we need to bring him back into the story. For example, we could simply end the chapter at the point where Beauman reaches for the pistol. Then in the following chapter we could flash back to fifteen years previously, when he was just beginning to make his fortune, and follow his life through to the point where he is about to commit suicide. After we show him finding the courage to change his mind, we can resume the story with his battle to clear his name and wreak revenge on his enemies.
- On the other hand, if you are aiming your story specifically at women, this could be the story of James Beauman's daughter—how she takes on impossible odds to prove her dead father's innocence. Again we would need to trace her father's background, for this would help show how his daughter has grown up in wealth and privilege.
- Another possible narrator for this story could be

a close male friend of the hero—who could end up romantically involved with his daughter.

Now you have a few ideas at least to start the wheels of your imagination rolling. Hopefully, you'll think of lots more. Whichever plotline you choose, of course, you'll have to figure out—and explain deftly to the reader—the details of the business predicament that led to the opening scenario.

CHAPTER 1

It was a voice she had never expected to hear again.

'Edith...You know who this is, don't you?'

She felt as if the blood had been sucked from her veins.

'You didn't think I'd forget, did you, Edith?'

The morning light streamed in through the drapes she had only just drawn back. The sound of the morning rush-hour traffic reached her faintly as her fingers froze around the receiver.

'I—' Her windpipe felt as if it had been clamped in a vise.

'You weren't counting on that, were you, Edith?'

Mesmerised, she heard the caller's low, taunting voice. And knew it was all over. Here. In the luxurious surroundings of the Plaza Hotel. At the moment of her greatest triumph.

'I've found you, Edith. And you know what that means, don't you?...My turn now...Perfect timing, wouldn't you agree? Or maybe, on second thoughts, you mightn't see it that way.' There was a mocking obscenity of a laugh and then the line went dead.

For a long, paralysing moment the woman who called herself Diana King stood listening to the hum of the disconnected line. Then the ice in her veins slowly gave way to a flood of molten lava.

Oh, God...not now...She fumbled the receiver back into its cradle. Please, oh please...not now...It was a silent, desperate plea to a God in whose justice and mercy she had long ago ceased to believe.

Turning stiffly, she looked with glazed, slate-blue eyes at the flower-filled suite, at the litter of the morning's first editions, at the Lacroix cream silk sheath dropped where she had stepped out of it the night before.

All evidence of her triumph. Her survival. A victory against all who had used and betrayed her. Hands curled into vicious fists, Diana King felt bitter tears well in her eyes and from her beautiful mouth came a low, terrible moan of animal pain.

Her dazzling, triumphant hour had been snatched away in a way she never would have imagined possible.

Why it works

Another good way of grabbing your readers' attention at the start of a story is by use of dialogue.

In this chapter, the opening sentence is loaded with intent. Immediately your readers should be asking themselves: Is this a good surprise or a bad one? A voice the woman wants to hear, or one that fills her with dread? And what is the message that voice is about to deliver?

By the third sentence we have given the answer. The voice at the other end of the line belongs to someone she is afraid of. And the dialogue and description that follow underline the character's fearful response.

In paragraph 8 we take the readers' suspense a little further by mentioning that 'it was all over', but keep them dangling by refusing to offer explanations. All the readers know at this point is that 'Edith' appears to be wealthy and successful. She's at the Plaza Hotel—perhaps the one in New York City—'at the moment of her greatest triumph'. And that information merely leads to more questions—which, in turn, helps hook our readers' attention.

Now we add another layer to the intrigue by revealing that 'Edith' now goes by the name of 'Diana King'. And we make it abundantly clear that the voice has shocked and terrified her. As we show her reaction, we also interweave hints to the extent of her success: the Lacroix gown, the flowers, the newspapers. Then in paragraph 13 we pick up on the suspense again, teasing the readers even more. Also note that at no stage do we let on whether the caller is male or female.

If this opening appeals to you, you could work at developing it into a full-length story by looking for answers to the following questions:

- Why has 'Edith' changed her name?
- At what has she just triumphed?
- Who has used and betrayed her, and why?
- Whose is the voice at the other end of the line?
- What is he or she capable of doing to her?

Always bear in mind that what gives a story momentum is a strong character with a substantial purpose or goal who is also facing major opposition.

Chapter One

The three mourners shivered at the graveside.

The grizzled, grey-haired priest muttered his way quickly through the funeral rites, eager to escape the bitterness of the bleak winter's afternoon. The cemetery stood on a bare, low hill and offered no protection from the icy winds that blew from the tundra to Poland's north.

The two elderly women pulled their dark shawls closer round their pasty peasant faces and suffered the stinging cold in stoical silence—as they had suffered so much in their hard lifetimes.

The man standing beside them did not share their resignation. He stamped his feet on the snowy ground and his dark eyes were restless, distracted, as the priest droned on.

Stefan Jankowski was 33 years old and determined to demand more from life than either his long-suffering mother or his aunt. The political upheaval that had taken place in Poland and the rest of the former Soviet bloc in the last few years meant little to the two elderly women. They didn't expect much to change in the short time left to them. Not for the better anyway.

But for Stefan Jankowski the future was suddenly bright with miraculous promise.

It had nothing to do with the fall of a corrupt and decayed regime. It had everything to do with the plain, blackwood coffin that lay on the hard, frozen ground at his feet.

Fresh snowflakes began to fall and Jankowski swore inwardly as he hunched himself deeper into his shabby overcoat. *Mother of God...how much longer...*

His gaze drifted to the horizon, to the line of immense wide-mouthed concrete chimneys that belched their poisonous gases into the leaden skies. Decades of unfettered industry had choked the air and poisoned the earth and rivers. The death rates spoke eloquently of the damage. Stefan's father, a miner since a boy, was buried just a short distance away, his life the ultimate sacrifice to the advancement of the state.

Now, as Stefan watched the sexton and his chapped-cheeked assistant lower the coffin into the toxic soil, he knew that for him the future was going to be different.

Despite the freezing wind, the stockily built Pole felt a warm glow of excitement flicker inside him. The problem of getting an exit visa was the only thing delaying him now. Those pigs of bureaucrats moved no faster just because their old masters had been removed.

Patience, he told himself. Patience just a little while longer.

Then, thanks to the woman whose remains lay in the cheap wooden coffin, all his dreams could finally come true.

Why it works

Let's see what we have told our readers in the opening sentences of this chapter. Someone has died. There are only three mourners, so he or she must be poor or unloved. The story is set in Poland. Those tidbits alone should be enough to intrigue readers, who will be wondering: Who has died? Why are there so few mourners? Are we in the period before or after the overthrow of Communist rule?

Paragraph 4 introduces one of the mourners, a man who we say is 'restless, distracted'. He doesn't seem to have much sympathy for the person being buried. So why is he at the funeral?

In the next paragraph we tell readers more about this character. He is Polish, young, from a peasant background but ambitious. The two other mourners are his mother and aunt. We also disclose that the story is set in the period following the breakup of the Soviet Union, and this should offer some interesting implications for our story. Why does the dead person offer Stefan intimations of a future 'suddenly bright with miraculous promise'? Could the 'political upheaval' have put secret police files into unauthorised hands? Has Stefan discovered something important about the person being buried? Something that he's convinced will change his whole life?

Whatever it is, we tell the readers immediately that Stefan is going to have to leave Poland to pursue his goal—and that the only thing delaying him is his exit visa. This will prompt more questions: Where is he headed? What does he know about the person in the coffin? Not until the last sentence do we reveal that this person is a woman. Now our readers can put all the clues together and start asking still more questions. It is these same questions that we will have to figure out answers to if we're to go on with the story:

- Is the dead woman related to Stefan?
- Has she always lived in Poland?
- Or has she come back to the country after the recent liberation?
- Has she spent her years abroad making a fortune in England, Australia or the US?

- How did she make her fortune?
- What secret did she carry with her that Stefan Jankowski might have discovered?
- How did he find it out? Was it told to him unwittingly by his mother or his aunt?
- Were they friends or relatives of the dead woman?
- Did they perhaps work for her?
- Did the dead woman die of natural causes? Or did Stefan have something to do with her death?

It should be clear by this stage that this character of dubious integrity can't be the 'hero' of the story, so you'll have to imagine how the storyline will develop so as to shift the focus to the heroine. She might be the dead woman's shunned daughter, given up at birth, whose quest to find out about her mother's past brings her into conflict with Stefan Jankowski.

It's up to you!

Chapter One

The sun shone warmly on the day Jack Lee was buried.

Since first light, representatives of the media had been taking up positions at the doors of Sydney's oldest Roman Catholic cathedral.

By the time the first mourners arrived, a huge and curious crowd stood sweating behind the long line of police barricades. But the promise of a riveting spectacle helped make the oppressive heat endurable.

A short time before the appointed hour the first of the convoy of sleek, dark limousines drew up at the doors of St Mary's and the assembled crowd pressed forward, eager to catch a glimpse of the country's rich and powerful.

As car followed car, politicians, industrialists and members of Australia's oldest and most respected families emerged sober-faced to pay their last respects to one of their country's wealthiest and most controversial figures. Even those who had hated the man were here.

From the final vehicle stepped a young woman, tall, fine-boned, a black lace mantilla covering her fair hair, her eyes hidden behind dark glasses.

With her elderly male companion hovering anxiously by her side, she made her way up the cathedral's wide stone steps, seemingly oblivious to the sea of faces, the whir of television cameras and the pop of flashbulbs.

Jenny Lee was 28. She had just inherited a fortune.

And it broke her heart.

The dusty venetian blinds were shut tightly against the late afternoon sunshine and only the flickering light from the outdated television set illumined the darkness.

The man sat tensely in the one easy chair, his naked back sticky against the worn green vinyl. Oblivious to the discomfort, he gulped from the beer can in his hand, his hard blue eyes never leaving the screen.

He watched the gleaming wooden casket being carried from the church, saw it slipped into the long, flower-filled hearse. Then the camera focus shifted to the girl.

With cold detachment the man watched as the

daughter of Jack Lee emerged from the church doors and moved towards the first of the line of waiting cars. Behind her he saw other well-known faces, their expressions arranged into appropriate solemnity for the bank of television cameras. A muscle twitched in his unshaven cheek and he took another mouthful of beer. If only they knew...

At that moment the ringing of the telephone broke the man's concentration. A spasm of anger shot through him, contorting his features as he crushed the now empty can in his thick, strong fingers.

Not now. He didn't want to miss a second of his triumph.

The ringing persisted, and for a moment he was tempted to ignore it. But then he remembered. He was important now. Perhaps he was needed again.

He lifted the receiver by his side and grunted a response. A moment later he broke into a smile. It broadened even further as he listened to the voice on the line, praising him for what he had done.

Why it works

Again we start our story with a funeral. But this one is very different. By the second sentence readers know that the dead man, Jack Lee, was a *somebody*. Cameras and reporters are present at his funeral as well as a huge crowd of onlookers. And the mourners are 'the country's rich and powerful'.

After showing how much Lee was apparently loved, in paragraph 5 we introduce a note of intrigue by telling our readers that this important man was also hated. And in the very next sentence we usher in our main character with a crisp description that can be expanded later. Then we again surprise our readers by giving them a quick insight into Jenny's point of view: inheriting her father's fortune, far from making her happy, has broken her heart.

Now our readers will be asking questions. Why is Jenny unhappy? Who was her father and why was he hated?

The second part of this chapter hints that maybe Jack Lee didn't die from natural causes. Was the unnamed man responsible? The mention of 'his triumph' certainly hints that he was. Yet the congregation of mourners don't appear to suspect foul play. Perhaps the man poisoned Lee. And, with the telephone call, we sow in the reader's mind the idea that he did not work alone.

In trying to extend this chapter into a complete storyline, let your imagination work on all the questions raised here.

- Why is Jenny heartbroken? Was she deeply attached to her father? Perhaps she was estranged from her father, and his death, as well as making her rich, has ended any possibility of reconciliation. If this is the case, we must also establish what caused the rift between father and daughter.
- Did Jenny alienate her father by trying to prove that she was more than just a rich man's daughter? Or did he reject her because he longed for a son to continue his empire?
- What was the basis of Jack Lee's fortune?
- On his deathbed did he wish to make up with his daughter, who arrived too late?
- Who would want Jack Lee dead? Who are his enemies? Perhaps they are even among those who are comforting his grieving daughter.
- Why did they want him dead? Perhaps he had aroused resentment and envy, or trampled on others, as he ruthlessly built his fortune.

Start thinking along these lines and you just might end up with a great story.

chapter one

For Margaret Vernon the day began like any other summer's day.

It was just before six when she stepped out onto the deck of her cliffside home, her perfectly maintained 39-year-old body wrapped in a brilliantly patterned silk sarong.

Heaven...Pure heaven...Margaret smiled to herself as she took in the glittering ocean lapping lazily onto the outrageously expensive curve of sand that was Sydney's Palm Beach.

This long-established summer retreat of Sydney's rich and powerful was less than an hour's drive north of the city, but for Margaret it was a lifetime away from the damp and dingy Manchester slum where she had spent her childhood.

On mornings like this, with the ocean sparkling diamond bright in the early sunshine and the rhythmic murmur of the breakers in her ears, the former Margaret Tobin would remember to bless the patron saint of ambitious women who had surely brought Keith Vernon into her life.

That miracle had occurred in London almost a dozen years ago, just when Margaret was beginning to feel the first stirrings of real panic about the future. It wasn't as if she hadn't done the groundwork—she'd worked hard on getting the right wardrobe, accent, address—but although she had spent her last penny in the process, her ultimate goal still remained frustratingly out of reach.

By the time of her fortuitous meeting with the Australian entrepreneur thirteen years her senior, Margaret had slept with an indefinite number of men—quite a few of whom hadn't even minded paying for the privilege. Yet time and time again the barrier of class had thwarted her ambitions. It was as if some indefinable hovering stench invariably alerted her prospective prey to the lowliness of her background.

But on that late June evening her luck had changed. A hard-won invitation to a smart dinner party at the honourable Arthur Neeson's Knightsbridge flat had provided the key to the door of her future.

Widowed just eight months, Keith Vernon had been on a business trip to London when he had accepted that fateful dinner invitation. For the 40-year-old businessman it was love at first sight when he was introduced to the fetching blonde in the low-cut dress which so perfectly matched her green eyes. They were seated across from each other at the long candle-lit table, and it didn't take Margaret long to sense the difference in his approach. Australians it seemed, were much less concerned about class than her fellow country-men. She could see the warm light of appreciation and desire in Keith Vernon's dark eyes. And in less time than it later took her to find Sydney on the map, she landed her prize.

The marriage took place a mere six months later beneath the arches of St Mark's church in Sydney's upmarket Darling Point. It was then the blushing bride got her first inkling that her husband's fellow citizens might not be quite as egalitarian as she had first surmised. Not all of the female guests were thrilled with the eligible widower's choice of wife. No doubt, Margaret told herself, they resented the fact that an outsider, and a Pom at that, had beaten them to such a desirable catch.

Yet she had seen no reason to let their antagonism worry her. Not with the gold and diamond ring on her left hand that proclaimed her Mrs Keith Vernon of Bellevue Hill and Palm Beach.

Slowly acceptance had come, and Margaret had settled into her adopted country with the ease of one who has found her spiritual home. She loved the summers at the beach. With Keith busy in the city all week she had the house to herself and enjoyed her solitude. She was never bored—she was too grateful for the ease and pleasure of her life.

Turning away from the view, Margaret went inside and prepared for her usual morning walk. At her heels her peach-coloured poodle, Dominique, pranced excitedly as she picked up her broad-brimmed raffia hat. She had seen what damage the sun could do in the complexions of her Australian contemporaries.

'Come on, then, Dommie.'

As they left the house Margaret followed the excited animal down the path through the trees that led to the beach. The sun on her arms felt like a sensual caress. Later it would grow fiercer, but by that time, she told herself, she would be safely ensconced inside with the latest magazines.

The sand was still cool beneath her bare feet as she headed towards the jutting headland with its unused lighthouse. Apart from a handful of surfboard riders far from the beach there were few people around at this hour. The real Christmas crowds—the holidaymakers who filled the apartments and caravan parks of the northern beaches—wouldn't be descending for another few days.

Margaret Vernon frowned at the thought. She'd grown as intolerant as her long-time neighbours to the intrusion of outsiders onto the strip of sand she had grown to regard as her own. Why couldn't the hordes find somewhere else to go with their litter and ice boxes and raucous ghetto blasters?

'Dommie! Come back here!' Lost in thought, she had allowed the little dog to wander too far away. Now she called again as she watched him scrambling over the dunes. He was still at the silly stage, she thought fondly. Just fourteen months old. Her sweet baby.

'Dommie!' She called again and clapped her hands until finally the dog bounded down the hills of sand towards her. As he came closer Margaret could see he was carrying something in his mouth. Now what...?

Then her mouth tightened. 'Dommie! Drop it! Drop it at once!'

Perhaps it was the rare sharpness of his mistress's tone that caused the dog to do as he was told. And with a look of disgust Margaret kicked sand over the used...well, they'd called them French letters in her youth. You'd think people would at least have the decency to dispose of the things properly. Kids, no doubt. In this climate, unlike Britain's, they could do it outside.

Margaret walked on with a frown. It was a wonder any local girls were still game enough for that sort of mischief after what had happened at Avalon, a couple of beaches down the coast. Twice now. And still the police hadn't come up with any likely suspects. Remembering the headlines, Margaret shivered despite the warmth of the sun.

But that was nothing to her reaction ten minutes later, when she arrived at the base of the headland.

She was picking her way through the sharp rocks when she saw it, a splash of colour floating gently in one of the tidal pools.

A lost towel, she guessed.

Until she got closer.

Why it works

As always, the mystery to come should be hinted at as early as possible. In this case we have done this in the first sentence. The implication is that while the day might have started like any other for Margaret Vernon, it didn't finish that way.

I don't envisage Margaret as the heroine of this story yet by exploring her background in this much detail we are establishing her an an important secondary character who could certainly reappear in the novel's later chapters.

By paragraph 3 we have also established the setting of our story: Palm Beach, Sydney, holiday haven of the rich and powerful. We need to be careful with less well-known settings such as this to explain where it's located. Note too that by paragraph 4 we have informed our readers that this enclave of wealth is not where Margaret Vernon grew up. To feed their inevitable curiosity about just how our character has managed to propel herself into such a different milieu, we tell our readers a little more about her: that as a girl she was desperate to find a wealthy husband. She single-mindedly refashioned all the aspects of herself that marked her lowly social class, but still had no luck—until she met Australian entrepreneur Keith Vernon. At this stage, we do not have to delve too deeply into her husband's background. To do that would slow down the story too much. And it is Margaret who is the focus of the action here. So we quickly trace Margaret's initial social difficulties in Australia and her ultimate acceptance by her husband's friends.

We can afford to give a fair bit of detail about Margaret here because we've already stirred our readers' curiosity about her. They'll read on because they still want to know why this particular day is going to end up being different from usual for her.

We link Margaret's current comfortable lifestyle with the opening moment of the story, where we find her standing looking at the view. Then we take her outside, where we disclose the first indication that all is not sunshine and roses in this wealthy retreat. When Margaret's pet poodle finds the used condom in the sand dunes, we use the character's thoughts to tell our readers that something disturbing has happened at Avalon (again, we explain its location) 'twice now'.

By not satisfying their curiosity about just what that might be, we give them another reason to keep turning the pages! And by hinting at the end of the chapter that Margaret has seen a body we let their imaginations work overtime.

Now yours must too, as you extend the story.

- Is the 'splash of colour' a body? In what state of decay is it? Clothed or unclothed? Is it a man, a woman, or a child?
- It might not be necessary to continue in Margaret's point of view. Instead, we could reveal more information by following the dialogue of the police when they arrive on the site, or later, as they discuss the murder among themselves—or by recounting the content of a news broadcast, perhaps referring

to a suspected link between this murder and earlier ones in the same area. Yet another way of offering the same information would be to have a group of other Palm Beach residents sitting around discussing the shocking news.

- Could the murderer actually be one of these people? A man or a woman? Could Margaret Vernon be an unwitting friend of the murderer?
- What would be a plausible motive for the murder. Could it perhaps be a copycat murder?
- Who is the victim? Another wealthy local? A child of one of Margaret's friends?
- What about the heroine of our story? Is she renting a place at Palm Beach for a few weeks over the summer? She might be a well-known local figure or perhaps an international high-flyer. Has she come to Palm Beach with a secret purpose?

Again, this opening hints at a cast of potentially interesting characters to play with. All you need to do is keep asking yourself questions—and finding answers. The more credible these are, the closer you will be to creating your own story.

chapter one

The girl refused to take no for an answer.

With growing impatience she repeated her request to the implacable secretary. But it was Anne Johannsen's job to filter out the time wasters. And the dangerous.

Not that she saw anything threatening in the exotic beauty who stood before her. Tall and willowy, with a thick curtain of dark, rippling hair, the girl was clearly Eurasian and her exotic features—the slightly slanted, luminous dark eyes and dramatic cheekbones, the small, straight nose and alabaster complexion—were stunning.

'It's impossible, I tell you,' the secretary repeated calmly. 'Ms Banks never sees unscheduled callers.' Then she added placatingly, 'Why don't you tell me what it's about and perhaps I can make an appointment for you—though I must warn you it won't be in the immediate future.'

The girl looked down at the middle-aged

woman at the desk and felt a sudden hot wave of anger. Did this crazy woman really think she was going to walk away now? After all this time?

She moved closer to the desk. 'I said I wanted to see Eve Banks—and I want to see her *now*.'

Anne Johannsen wasn't easily intimidated. But an involuntary shiver ran down her spine as those fierce, glittering dark eyes met her own. Suddenly, doubting her earlier judgment, she wondered if she should use the security button placed discreetly at the base of her desk. A necessary precaution when one worked for a woman as controversial as Eve Banks.

'Look, I've tried to tell you. It's not possible—'

The girl interrupted, her voice barely under control.

'Then do this for me. Give this to your boss.' She took a long, sealed envelope from the cheap raffia bag slung over her shoulder. 'Then if she says she does not wish to see me I will go.'

Anne Johannsen pursed her lips in annoyance as the girl dropped the envelope on the desk in front of her. What the hell...Demanding little vixen...Still, it might be the only way to get rid of her short of calling security.

With a curt nod she rose from her desk and, aware of the girl's silent scrutiny, crossed the room and tapped at the door to the inner office.

Eve Banks was on the telephone, speaking in her usual quickfire fashion. She looked up with an inquisitive frown as her secretary passed the envelope across the cluttered desk and gestured at the reception area.

Still speaking, Eve cradled the receiver against her thick brown hair and carefully tore open the envelope. A split second later her green eyes grew wide in astonishment and she stopped speaking in mid-sentence. The blood iced in her veins as she looked at the hand-written pages.

It was impossible...totally impossible...

Why it works

This time our story opens with an immediate suggestion of conflict—always a good way to catch readers' attention. We also hint at the intrigue to come by referring to 'the dangerous'. The implication here is that the girl is somehow a potential threat to our heroine.

In paragraph 2 we give a name to the secretary. This tells our readers that she's not going to be a minor character in the story. A clearly drawn secondary character is always useful as a confidante for the heroine. And who better for Eve Banks to confide in than her loyal, trustworthy secretary? This character will enable us to impart key information, not only by tracing the heroine's thoughts, but in active scenes and dialogue between her and her confidante.

In paragraph 7 we work on building a sense of danger by referring to the 'security button' and telling our readers that this hard-to-visit heroine is 'controversial'. Even before bringing Eve Banks into the scene, we have thus given readers just enough pertinent information about her to arouse their curiosity.

In paragraph 3 we quickly sketch a description of the girl—establishing the fact that she is Eurasian.

- Who is the girl? Is she part Chinese? Can we tie the story into Hong Kong's handover to China? Or is she Vietnamese? Perhaps she has some knowledge about our heroine's brother, who has been missing in action since the end of the war.
- Why is she a threat? She could be Japanese, with some link to the Yakuza—the Japanese Mafia.
- What is our heroine's occupation? How might what she does be related to the fact that the girl has sought her out?
- What is in the mysterious envelope? A leaked political document? A letter from her missing brother? The details of a murder? In finding answers to these questions you will develop a strong motivation for the heroine and at the same

time place her in a position of conflict. Because don't forget, if you haven't got a conflict, you haven't got a story.

CHAPTER ONE

MOBILE, ALABAMA, early 1990s.

'This time a bullet's not going to be enough!'

Thomas Carmichael looked at his colleagues through a mist of fine Havana cigar smoke. All three were nodding in silent agreement. Not one of them underestimated the magnitude of the problem.

The meeting of the two right-wing senators, the millionaire property developer and the newspaper magnate was taking place in the utmost secrecy. Each had arrived separately at the Carmichael mansion on the outskirts of Mobile, their identities hidden behind the tinted windows of air-conditioned limousines.

The four, all in their 60s, had known each other for many years. Yet friendship was not a term to which any of them affixed meaning. Rather, they shared a common bond. It was that which had led to this emergency meeting.

Thomas Carmichael, triple chins resting on his

shirt front, took a long swallow of bourbon from his crystal tumbler. He spoke dispassionately. 'King was taken care of, Jackson failed twice, but this sonofabitch Warner is getting too close for fuckin' comfort.'

'He's gonna make it, Tom. Plain as the dollar signs in a whore's eye—if we don't come up with somethin'.'

Senator Clive Wyman's slow, rolling speech revealed his Louisiana ancestry. A thin, pale-faced man with a fringe of reddish hair and a perpetually aggrieved expression, he had a vulpine instinct for survival that had kept him in Washington for over twenty years.

'Ain't gonna be easy.' Harvey Giles put down his empty glass on the parquetry table by his elbow. A thickset, beetle-browed man who had made his fortune building half of Atlanta, he had a deceptively laconic manner, which hid a quick, savage temper and a mind as sharp as a tack.

But close as he was to Tom Carmichael, even he had no idea what the newspaper magnate had in mind.

''Course it ain't gonna be easy! But nothin's gonna make me sit back while a nigger gets elected President of this goddamn country!' Ed Quinn's tone overflowed with hatred. A

Republican Senator for Alabama, he was a long-standing champion of ultra-conservative whites.

Cigar clamped between his thick, protruding lips, Carmichael looked at the anxious faces around him. He was savouring his moment of triumph. Heny Giles, Clive Wyman, Ed Quinn—all, he knew, considered themselves shrewd, quick-thinking operators. But none of them could have come up with the spectacular solution that he had worked out. But then, he thought, exhaling a stream of smoke, he probably had more damn reason…

Not that any of them would be aware of that.

'Gentlemen.' His smile was smug. 'Y'all better get ready to kiss my ass…Cause what I got figured out's gonna get rid of all our problems in the one mind-blowin' hit…'

Two hours later, when the meeting was over, none of those present doubted that Mobile, Alabama, would be a name the world would ever forget.

DALTRY HILL, ALABAMA, 1946.

'Surely you're not ailin', honey? Not on a day like this?'

Sevres china teacup halfway to her lips, Mrs Amelia Danville looked anxiously at her eldest daughter across the lace-topped breakfast table.

CHAPTER ONE

Charlotte Danville, eyes cast downwards, shook her head. 'No, Mamma, it's...it's just the heat.'

With a smile, Amelia visibly relaxed. 'Well, you would choose August to come into this world, Charlotte, darling.' She took a sip of tea, placed the fine bone cup back in its saucer and pressed the damask napkin delicately to her lips. 'Twenty-one years ago today...Oh, my, it's hard to believe.'

She gave her tall, slender daughter an admiring look, taking in the glossy, wavy hair that tumbled half way down her back, the lovely, heart-shaped face and the dark, luminous eyes. There was no doubting Charlotte was a beauty, she thought. So much like herself as a young woman, if she wanted to be immodest. But so different in personality. At 21, Amelia remembered, she'd been nothing but carefree and light-hearted. Not serious and earnest like Charlotte. The girl could be so difficult sometimes. Stubborn, too. Once she got an idea in her head no one could budge her.

But, Amelia reassured herself, Thomas would be able to handle her. She was sure of that. After all, hadn't he and Charlotte grown up together? Played together as children? The match between them had been practically inevitable. And Amelia knew the Carmichaels were every bit as pleased as she was with the engagement that would make this evening a double celebration.

Every time she thought about it, her heart raced with excitement. The Carmichaels were one of Alabama's oldest, wealthiest families and the wedding was certain to be the social event of the year. Amelia just loved the prospect of all the planning and organising.

A moment later her thoughts were interrupted by her younger daughter. 'I just can't wait for tonight, Mamma! It's going to be so much fun!'

Amelia turned her smile to Madeline, who was tucking into her usual hearty breakfast. At sixteen, dear Maddy still had to emerge from her puppy fat but the Danville good looks had been lavished on her, too, with her dark tumble of curls, sweet blue eyes and glowing complexion. And thankfully, Amelia thought, in contrast to Charlotte's cool reserve Maddy was effusive and spontaneous. The boys flocked around her in droves. Amelia felt sure that her younger daughter wouldn't wait until she was 21 to catch herself the right man and settle down.

As she poured syrup over another flapjack, Maddy gave her elder sister an appraising look. 'You don't seem real excited, Charrie. I'd be just c-razy about getting engaged to a man as handsome and exciting as Thomas Carmichael.'

Charlotte Danville felt her stomach tighten at

the mention of her fiancé's name. Abruptly she pushed back her chair and rose to her feet.

'May I be excused, Mamma? I'm going to take Button out for a while.'

A frown drew Amelia's fine brows together. 'Now mind you don't tire yourself, Charlotte. This is a very special day and you've got to store up the energy to enjoy it.'

Charlotte murmured a reply as she left the breakfast room. She was trying not to think too much about tonight. But as she called for the small, excited terrier to follow her out of the house she couldn't help but dwell on her sister's comments. It was true, she thought, she didn't feel excited about this evening. And yet she couldn't say why. Surely a girl should feel blissfully happy when she was about to become engaged to one of the state's most eligible bachelors? For Tom Carmichael was certainly that—a scion of one of Alabama's wealthiest families, owners of the prestigious *Alabama Chronicle.*

Most of her friends, Charlotte knew, were green with envy that she was the one who had been chosen to bear the title of Mrs Thomas Carmichael. And Thomas was so good to her, so charming, so generous.

So why, she asked herself yet again, did she feel

so—uneasy? So full of trepidation? What was the matter with her?

Lost in her troubled thoughts, she headed across the lawn towards the river that ran in sluggish siltiness around the perimeter of the Danville estate. The trees that shaded her had been planted by her great-grandfather when he'd purchased these 50 or so acres from the profits of his rapidly expanding retail empire. By the time he had found a bride, he had also been wealthy enough to build the rambling mansion that, with its towers and pillars and turrets, so resembled the grand homes of Europe.

Now, as she strolled, Charlotte caught sight of the activity on the green lawns behind the house. Coloured lights were being strung between the trees, the gardeners were putting the finishing touches to the flower beds, and teams of coloured helpers were setting up tables in the marquee. Her mother had started organising the engagement party almost the moment she'd been told the good news.

Charlotte felt a sudden dryness in her mouth as she reached the cool shade of the willows. She should be so happy, ecstatic. Tom was her friend. They had known each other for years. At 26 he was handsome, confident, wealthy and well-connected. And he loved her, Charlotte was sure about that. He was always telling her so.

'We'll be one of Alabama's finest couples, sweetest. The newspaper will keep me busy all week but we'll have the most marvellous weekends. I know you'll make a wonderful hostess. Not to mention wife and mother, of course.'

He had kissed her then, his lips firm but chaste upon her cheek. But Charlotte was aware of his quickened breathing, understood the desire he was fighting so hard to control until their wedding night.

And maybe, she told herself, that's when she would feel it too. Perhaps when they were man and wife the fire would catch hold, the fire she had read about, been told about in whispers by her married friends. The passion that made a woman feel and do the things she would never otherwise dream of...

Only what, Charlotte wondered fearfully, if it doesn't happen even then? What if even knowing that she was Tom's legal wife didn't manage to change this deadness, this coldness at the core of her?

Her eyes swam with sudden tears. What's wrong with me? Why can't I feel what I'm supposed to feel? she thought.

Swallowing hard, she made an effort to push

the nightmarish doubts from her mind. It would be all right. It had to be.

'Button!' She suddenly realised that the little dog was snuffling excitedly among the tree roots on the riverbank. 'Button! Come here!'

But the animal ignored her call, his little head down, his front paws scrabbling away at the earth. Why, he'd be filthy, Charlotte thought, and her mother would be angry that one of the servants would have to waste precious time, today of all days, carting the little rascal off for a bath.

Reaching into the pocket of her dress she produced the small rubber ball she'd brought with her. Holding it aloft, she called again, 'Look, Button! Come and chase!'

The enticement did the trick. The terrier's head shot up and a moment later he was scampering towards her as fast as his short legs could carry him. He leapt in delight as Charlotte threw the ball, and within seconds he was back, dropping the plaything at his mistress's feet, barking at her to repeat this wonderful game.

Charlotte obliged, vaguely aware of being observed by some of the coloured workers who were part of the small army of extra staff her mother had recruited for the evening. It was going to be the biggest party they'd ever thrown at Daltry Hill. Everyone would be there...

CHAPTER ONE

Lost again in her troubled thoughts, Charlotte continued throwing the ball. She knew Button was capable of playing this particular game until totally exhausted.

Then it happened. In the frantic effort of the chase the terrier accidentally knocked the rubber ball into the nearby stream. Unhesitatingly he launched himself after it, paddling furiously in pursuit, but the eddying tide only carried the plaything further out of his reach.

As Charlotte watched in dismay, her tiring pet made for a small sandbank in the middle of the swirling, muddy water. There he struggled out, shook his bedraggled fur, then looked expectantly at his mistress. Come and get me, his whole demeanour beseeched.

Charlotte gave an exasperated moan. 'Oh, Button! You dumb mutt...Come on, you'll have to swim out of there.' But to her chagrin the tiny animal's only response was a loud whimpering as he began to circle in frustration. It was obvious he had no intention of re-entering the water.

From where she stood on the bank, Charlotte bit her lip in annoyance. She saw quite clearly what she'd have to do. The river wasn't particularly deep. If she was careful she could easily rescue her naughty pet. But it was sure going to make a mess of her dress. For a moment she wondered if she should go back to the house for help. But she decided against it. She couldn't leave Button here to fret alone.

Slipping off her shoes, she gathered up the hem of her full-skirted cotton dress and waded slowly into the muddy water. To the accompaniment of the little dog's excited squeals she moved carefully forward, her eyes searching out the shallowest points to place her feet.

It took her only a few moments to reach the sandbank and she scooped the trembling, wet animal into her arms.

'Okay, okay.' Button squirmed in delight as she tucked him under one arm and stepped back into the stream. 'Steady on, you crazy mutt, or you'll have us both in the water.'

No sooner were the words out of her mouth than her next step plunged them both into one of the stream's deep holes.

Charlotte could swim but she was hampered by trying to keep her grip on the frightened, squirming animal in her arms. Scrambling desperately to reach higher ground, she felt herself being sucked down by the weight of her dress and petticoats.

Oh, God...She tried to scream for help but coffee-coloured water filled her mouth, her nostrils...Kicking desperately, she surfaced, gulped precious air and felt herself being dragged under again.

It was then that the crazy thought spun into her head. She was about to die. On her 21st birthday she was going to die...

Just as she began sinking, overwhelmed by panic and dread, she felt strong arms encircle her, lifting her head firmly above the murky water.

'It's okay...I've got you. Just relax.'

Her rescuer was speaking close to her ear as he dragged them both backwards to the safety of the riverbank. A moment later Charlotte felt her feet touch the sandy bottom and then those same strong arms were helping her up the steep, slippery bank. Only then did she thankfully release her grip on the squirming dog and sink down on the rough grass beneath the trees, panting for breath.

'You okay?'

Charlotte nodded as she gulped air into her lungs. Then for the first time she lifted her head to look at her rescuer. Her eyes widened in surprise as they met the concerned gaze of a man with a strong-boned, perfectly shaped face. A dark face.

'I...thank you. Thank you so much. My dog...got stuck out there. I was trying to bring him back when I slipped.'

'I heard the splash and thought I'd better check.'

'Lucky for me you did.' Suddenly Charlotte became acutely aware of the way her dress was clinging damply to her body. With an attempt at aplomb she said, 'I guess—I'd better get back to the house.'

'Here, let me help you up.' He stood in front of her, his hand outstretched, and as Charlotte looked up she felt her cheeks suddenly heat at the sight of the strong, athletic torso revealed by his clinging T-shirt.

'Th—thank you.' Their hands met. His grip was strong, firm, and as she saw the muscles ripple in his smooth dark arms, she suddenly felt as if her breath had been cut off.

Only when they were safely on the path at the top of the bank did he release his hold.

'If you're okay, I guess I'd better be gettin' back to work. There's still a lot to do yet.'

As she stared back into those intense eyes Charlotte felt a strange shiver go through her. His height, his looks, the unusual lack of subservience in his tone and manner...everything about the man who stood before her was overpowering.

And then something, she wasn't sure what, made her volunteer: 'It's my party tonight. My

21st birthday.' And immediately wondered why she hadn't said it was her engagement party too…

He smiled a slow smile. A perfect smile. 'You're Miss Danville?'

Charlotte nodded, her arms clutched around her chest in an attempt at modesty. 'And your name?' she asked, her shyness giving a peremptory edge to her tone.

'Hal Warner, Ma'am.'

'Thank you again then, Hal. Now I think I'd better go and change.'

And turning away from that dark, disconcerting gaze she made her hurried way back to the house.

Back to the fate that awaited her.

Across the river where the drive led through the trees to the house, a man had brought his open-roofed car to a sudden halt. He had arrived just in time to witness the aftermath of the rescue. Now, as he restarted the engine, his blue eyes blazed in his handsome face and his knuckles clenched white around the leather-covered steering wheel. With a spin of the rear wheels, Thomas Carmichael continued on towards the Danville mansion.

'And don't those two just look the per-fect couple, Amelia?'

Face flushed, blue eyes glowing, Lana

Carmichael turned to where her son's future mother-in-law sat beside her on the lantern-lit terrace.

Amelia nodded as she looked down to where Charlotte and Thomas stood hand in hand on the lawn surrounded by their friends. Gusts of raucous laughter floated upwards on the warm evening air and it occurred to Amelia that perhaps there'd been a touch too much hard liquor in the punch.

'It'll be a good match, Lana. Thomas will bring out the best in Charlotte, I'm sure.' Amelia waved away a pesky mosquito. The night had gone exactly as she'd planned—the dinner, the speeches, the dancing. But, she mused in happy anticipation, the wedding would be her *pièce de résistance.*

'Thomas is crazy about her. Always has been, ever since he was old enough to know what a girl was.' Lana Carmichael patted her friend's arm, noting the sparkle of a diamond bracelet she had never seen before.

'You and Zachary have done a wonderful job, Amelia. Charlotte's a credit to you both. You've educated her, shown her the world, taught her the fear of the Lord. She'll make Thomas a wonderful wife.'

Amelia smiled. 'That'll make both of us happy, then, Lana. Now,' she gestured towards the house, 'why don't you and I go indoors and see what the menfolk are up to?'

It was still there inside her, eating at her.

As Charlotte moved with Thomas among their guests, accepting the kisses and warm words of congratulation, her sense of unease grew stronger by the moment.

She was filled with the dreadful sensation that she was playing a role in some theatrical production. The role of the happy, smiling fiancée whose future was marked out with joyous certainty.

Except that beneath the façade the real her existed, the young woman who felt as if she were suffocating, drowning in emotional turmoil, the Charlotte who kept wondering if she really loved enough the man who had asked her to become his wife.

But it was too late now, she told herself. Too late for doubts. What would it do to her mother's wonderful plans for the wedding? To Thomas and his dreams for the future?

Pull yourself together, she chided herself as she stood by Thomas's side under one of the magnificent firs that had been dotted with coloured lights. Any other girl here tonight would give her eye teeth to be marrying Thomas Carmichael. She was being just plain stupid to think...

It was then she saw him, coming towards her through the trees, a tray of freshly filled glasses in his hands.

Instantly, Charlotte felt her heart lurch in her chest. Her head swam with a momentary giddiness. Even dressed in serving attire Hal Warner exuded a powerful presence.

And suddenly he was beside her, offering her a drink, his dark, luminous eyes intent upon her.

'You okay now, Miss Danville?' He asked the question quietly.

Charlotte nodded, found the breath to speak. 'Yes. Thank you. No ill effects, as you can see.'

'I'm glad. No girl'd want to miss her engagement party.' His eyes still held hers and she felt the heat glow in her cheeks.

'No—'

'You doin' your job, boy?'

It was Thomas. Standing close beside her. And using a tone Charlotte had never heard before.

'Yes, sir.' Hal Warner spoke to Thomas as he had spoken to Charlotte. Polite, but without the deferential note of a servant.

'That's funny. I coulda sworn I heard you havin' a conversation with Miss Danville, here. You're not lyin' to me, are you boy?'

The taunt and aggression in Thomas Carmichael's voice were unmistakable. While

Charlotte looked on in dismay, he took a step closer to the man holding the tray.

'Tom...' Charlotte quickly laid a restraining hand on her fiancé's arm. But roughly he shrugged it off.

'No, Charlotte, it seems to me this nigger here is far too familiar with his betters for his own good.'

'Tom, please,' Charlotte's heart raced as she interjected. 'I told you. This is the man who pulled me out of the river this afternoon. He was only asking—'

Her fiancé threw her a glance. His face was set, his mouth a hard line. 'Sure, you told me, Charlotte...but does that give the nigger a right to annoy you when you're with your guests? Or,' he was staring contemptuously now into Hal Warner's dark face, 'is he lookin' for another chance to put his hands all over you?'

'Tom!' Face ashen, Charlotte looked at him in shock. Around them, conversation had ceased as nearby guests took in the tense scene.

Why it works

Well, what do you think about this one? Plenty to get your teeth into? I hope you can see some real possibilities in the range of interesting characters presented here.

Let's take a closer look at the techniques we've used to make this opening chapter irresistible to readers.

First, we have a confronting opening sentence that immediately spells violent conflict. And within a couple more sentences we tell our readers these four men have a major problem on their hands—and, we quickly see, are intent on solving it by some evil means.

When several characters are introduced at once, it's important to give each some distinctive characteristic that will fix him in readers' minds. Let's see how we've done that here.

To begin with, we have wasted no time in setting out the identities of the men: two right-wing senators, a millionaire property developer and a newspaper magnate are certainly a very rich and powerful coalition.

Next, we describe each man in a quick pen picture: Tom Carmichael smokes Havanas and is very fat. Senator Clive Wyman has the 'slow, rolling speech' of his Louisiana ancestry, is thin, red-haired and pale-faced, and has a 'perpetually aggrieved expression'. He's also clearly a force to be reckoned with. Harvey Giles is stocky and heavy-browed, with a 'quick, savage temper and a mind as sharp as a tack'.

Ed Quinn's physical appearance can be left until later. What's more important for our readers to know is that he hates 'niggers' and is 'a longstanding champion of ultra-conservative whites'. Thus, in these few paragraphs, we have given readers just enough information about our characters to establish mood and motive.

We've made a lot of use of dialogue, too, to pinpoint the men's attitudes and political views. At the same time, we have tried not to give too much play to regional accents or odd turns of phrase, which can both distract and irritate readers. From now on, we may use just the odd colloquial idiom to remind readers of the characters' origins.

Bearing in mind that it's looking for the answers to questions that keep readers turning the pages, let's take note of the questions that we have implicitly posed in the opening paragraphs: What is the problem facing this group of men? Why the secrecy of the 'emergency' meeting? What bond do they share?

Clearly these men are hostile towards blacks despite the gains of the civil libertarians. By paragraph 5 their antagonism and the depths of their concern about rising black political power are made abundantly clear. Martin Luther King and Jesse Jackson might have failed to gain real political power, but it seems that another black man named Warner is now too close to success for the comfort of these white Southerners.

This leads naturally into paragraph 6, where we supply at least the germ of our characters' motive for the meeting. They've got to 'come up with somethin''—to stop Warner, presumably. And a few paragraphs on, we let the readers know that Thomas Carmichael has already worked out a 'spectacular solution', and add extra intrigue by suggesting that Carmichael probably had more reason than the others to do so. But once again, we give no further detail here in the hope that curiosity will keep our readers glued to the page! The only hint we let slip is that, whatever Carmichael's solution, it's going to have worldwide impact (paragraph 14).

That amounts to a good deal of detail and information in just a few paragraphs. But shoehorning it all in without boring our readers is never an easy task. It can take hours of work shaping the opening section so that information is unfolded gradually and smoothly, leaving readers barely aware of how many clues they're being offered. Such skill comes only with practice.

The next part of the story, set in the 1940s, would probably work better as a separate chapter. I have included it here as an example of how to move from Chapter One into the rest of the story.

Having set the present-day scene and outlined all

its tensions to grab readers' attention, we now use flashback to fill in the background that will link up later to our opening chapter. As I've said before, it's always best to whet readers' appetites first—even if it means entering the story in mid-plot—so that they'll be happy to absorb the detail that is required to tell the rest of the story.

To begin, we again give a minimum of detail to paint the scene: the fine china, indicating a well-to-do household; the facts that it's August and Charlotte Danville's 21st birthday. In paragraph 19 we again introduce Thomas Carmichael, this time as a young man, and disclose that he's about to get engaged to Charlotte Danville, with whom he has grown up.

This information is imparted via the thoughts of Amelia Danville, Charlotte's mother, rather than through the omniscient and more distant author's voice. By entering a character's thoughts we make our story more immediate and personal. Through Amelia's musings we can tell the reader much about the Carmichael family and her delight that her daughter is marrying into such a prestigious clan.

Paragraph 23 introduces Maddy, Charlotte's younger sister, and draws a contrast between the two girls. Again, remember to dwell only on those characters you are going to use later in your story. There'd be no point in introducing Maddy if she wasn't going to be important in some way to the plot. You might already have started musing on the possibilities: Will she be Charlotte's confidante? Or will she end up being her rival at some later stage? Will she die, perhaps? How? Whose fault will it be? Alternatively, would it be better to rewrite this scene and give Charlotte a brother? A boy who hates Thomas Carmichael and can't accept the idea of his sister's marriage to him? This could be a useful source of conflict in the rest of the story.

In paragraph 24 we tell the reader, this time through Maddy's eyes, that Charlotte is not very excited about her engagement. And this leads naturally into Charlotte's own thoughts on that matter. In the next few paragraphs we show Charlotte's confusion about her engagement to Thomas and also provide more information about the Danvilles. In a few sentences we sketch in how the family made their money and paint a quick picture of the home built by Charlotte's great-grandfather. Subtly, we are filling readers in on our story's background without delivering it in one indigestible lump.

Everything that happens in our story must happen for a reason. By having Charlotte walk her little dog, we lead naturally into the drama of her narrow escape from drowning (which, of course, we can't allow to happen because Charlotte is our heroine!) and her rescue by Hal Warner. This is a crucial scene, for it establishes Hal as a strong potential love interest by showing Charlotte's reaction to his good looks and intense gaze. But it also tells readers a lot about Hal. The 'lack of subservience in his tone' immediately sets him apart from the usual servant.

Dramatic as the rescue and meeting are, we can get still more value out of them with the hint of more drama to come, which we achieve by having Thomas Carmichael—unseen by Hal and Charlotte—witness the aftermath of the rescue. His furious reaction prompts readers to expect a later confrontation between the two men.

Instead of following the three characters on their separate ways, we could now jump a bit further along in the story and show our readers that very confrontation. But before we enter that dramatic moment, we lower our readers' expectation that this will happen soon and create a lull in which the two mothers-in-law discuss the success of the evening's party. After a further few paragraphs that reveal Charlotte's continuing unease at the idea of marriage to Thomas, we now surprise our readers by describing, in rapid succession, Charlotte's unexpected meeting with Hal Warner, the effect it has on her, and the hostile exchange between Hal and Thomas, which reveals more about the characters of the two men.

The scenario offered here should give you plenty to muse on as you work out a storyline. Remember, you will figure out your plot by asking yourself the same questions that readers ask when they're reading your story:

- Will Charlotte marry Thomas or will she shock everyone by eloping with Hal? If she elopes, what difficulties will the couple face? How will Thomas Carmichael react? Is he driven by hate of Hal Warner and the woman who jilted him?

You will also have to ask questions about the opening of the story. It appears to indicate that one of Hal's sons is in the running for the presidency.

- How did he get to that position?
- What will happen to him?
- What has happened to Charlotte and Hal in the 40 or so years since they met?

As you try to find answers to these questions you will not only stretch your imagination but very likely come up with a wonderful story.

chapter one

The interruption could not have been more badly timed.

For more than three hours Armand Kessler had been dealt lousy hand after lousy hand. Finally, he was poised to end his losing streak. As befitted a man who had painstakingly plotted his way through the bureaucratic jungle to become chief of police of Switzerland's second-largest city, his pale, pudgy face betrayed no sign of emotion as he looked down at his royal flush.

But his luck was out that evening. Just as he was about to call the bluff of that liverish oaf who ran the city's most profitable brothel, there was a knock on the door, and with an apologetic cough a uniformed sergeant poked his head into the smoke-filled room.

'Herr Kommandant, forgive me, please...but something urgent...'

'*Ja, ja*,' the police chief snapped. A pot of almost three months' salary was at stake. Why did he have to be interrupted now? 'What is it, Gruber? It had better be worth the disturbance, man.'

The young detective sergeant looked nervous. 'Uh…if we could speak in private, *mein Herr*?'

With a heavy sigh, Armand Kessler lifted an apologetic shoulder to his waiting companions. Placing his precious cards down carefully on the blanket-covered table, he heaved his ponderous bulk out of the chair. 'A moment, gentlemen, *bitte*.'

He shut the door sharply behind him, his bad temper obvious. The hallway of the small hotel where the regular weekly card game took place was deserted. But still the nervous sergeant felt compelled to whisper his message.

As he listened to the details, the police chief's face grew paler. No…surely not…It was impossible….Then he spat out a vicious stream of invective against the Lord, His mother and even some of the saints.

For Armand Kessler knew without a doubt that he had just lost all chance of playing his winning hand that night.

Why it works

You'll note that again in this chapter, it's not the protagonist who opens the story. Nonetheless, our character should hold readers' attention for at least two reasons: he's the chief of police, and he's involved in a poker game which has just turned his way.

In this opening, we've used a new way to breathe life into a character. In this instance we give no physical description at all of Armand Kessler. Instead, we tell readers who he's playing cards with. That his opponents include the city's most profitable brothel owner should immediately reveal that this is no by-the-book cop.

Having focused on Kessler here, we're pretty certain he will come into our story later on. But we haven't given so much detail about him that we can't afford to drop him later. Perhaps he is here merely as a device to introduce a dramatic event that kicks off our plot.

How do we let on that something important has occurred? The detective sergeant looks nervous; he has to talk to his boss in private; he whispers his message even when there is very little chance that he will be overheard. Once again, though, to maximise suspense, we don't immediately tell readers what has happened. All they are told is that Kessler's face has grown pale and that he has lost all chance that night of playing his winning hand.

Now ignite your imagination. Ask yourself:

- What has happened to so disturb the chief of police? The murder or assassination of a prominent citizen? A bomb threat? Sabotage in an Alpine road tunnel? A mistress reporting the death *in flagrante* of her lover, who is a high-profile judge or politician? The escape from jail of a notorious criminal?

In seeking answers to your questions, you'll find that more questions will be posed. Slowly, steadily, as you deal with each one in turn, the plot of your story should begin to form.

Chapter One

The woman emerged from the clinic and stood for a moment on the sidewalk as if unsure where to head next.

Her narrow face was pale and drawn and she shivered in the chill drizzle that was already frizzing her short brown hair. She'd been gone so long, she thought, she'd almost forgotten the bite of the English cold.

Despite the rain, Rebecca decided to walk. Her hotel wasn't that far away—and she was still fit enough for that. But more than anything else, she needed time to think. To comprehend the news that had just been so delicately but unequivocally relayed to her.

In truth, it hadn't really come as a shock. For almost a year now the pains had come and gone. Sharp and severe, they would hit without warning but had always subsided eventually. Until these last few weeks. That was when she knew she would have to do something more than rely on the aloof assurance of the doctor she'd visited in Majorca, the cool, patrician Spaniard who, after barely bothering to examine her, had diagnosed her problem as 'mere gastric upset' of the type common among tourists faced with unfamiliar diets.

But Rebecca Weir wasn't a tourist. She had lived in Majorca for almost four years, scratching out a living, enduring the indifference of an audience who talked and laughed or, worse still, heckled drunkenly as she took the stage every evening.

Occasionally her name would strike a chord and someone in the mainly British audience would come up after the show and say how much they'd loved her 'in the old days'. Meaning, of course, when they were both young, when they'd all had hopes and dreams, when anything was possible. Rebecca could see the pity in the eyes of some. The sympathy for someone who might have made it big but who was now reduced to earning her living in third-rate foreign bars.

As Rebecca walked the wet pavements of London, the city where she had arrived so young and so full of wild dreams, bitter tears welled in her eyes. She *could* have made it too, she thought defiantly, but the dream had been snatched away by what had happened.

And from that time on she had paid the price. Wherever she had run—Miami, Rome, Johannesburg—she'd never been able to escape. The suspicion and the guilt had followed her everywhere, eaten her inside, and in the end, she felt sure, contributed to the disease that she'd just learned would soon take her life at 42.

At once, hot panic fluttered in her throat. Four weeks, the specialist had told her. So little time to try to put things right. To right that terrible wrong.

But that didn't mean she wasn't going to try.

Why it works

This story opens in a rather low key way. But in two short paragraphs we still manage to give our readers quite a lot of information. The word that should leap out at once is 'clinic'. That immediately conjures up trouble for this character, and sets readers wondering: is she mentally ill? a drug addict? Has she just had an abortion or other operation?

Before we dole out any answers, we next give a brief description of the character, establish the location as England, and tell readers that the heroine has been away from there a long time. The reference to her feeling the cold suggests that she has been living in a warmer climate, which should lead readers to wonder not only where, but also why she has returned to England.

By paragraph 3 we are ready to prod the intrigue a little further. Now we tell our readers that Rebecca is 'still fit enough' to walk the distance to her hotel. That, along with the reference to the 'clinic', hints at a serious health problem, which is emphasised by Rebecca's need of 'time to think', to 'comprehend the news' she has been given at the clinic.

In paragraphs 4 and 5 we answer the question of where she has been and for how long. We also confirm readers' suspicions that Rebecca is facing a serious health crisis, noting that her problem has been dogging her for some time—and that a Spanish doctor has failed to cure it.

Note how each paragraph that follows adds a little bit more to the profile of our character: gradually we reveal that she is an entertainer 'scratching out a living' before drunken crowds of mainly British tourists. Through the character's own thoughts we convey her bitterness at never having had the chance to fulfil her potential. Her failure, we suggest, is no fault of her own, but the result of 'what had happened'.

By now you'll have learned enough about the use of suspense and intrigue to know that we're not going to be telling what *that* is just yet! All we do reveal is that whatever did happen to Rebecca caused her to run away from England—to Rome, Miami, Johannesburg—but that it was no good; 'the suspicion and guilt had followed her everywhere' and have been so corrosive that they have very likely caused the disease that (we now disclose) is going to kill her.

That might lay us open to accusations of telling our readers how the story will end. To overcome this, though, we let them know that a great deal is going to happen between now and then, for Rebecca is going to use that time to try to 'right that terrible wrong'.

Again, in a dozen or so short paragraphs, we have raised many questions. In addition, we have established two fundamentals that give a story momentum—strong motivation, and a race against time.

Now see if you can take things to their conclusion. That means more questions, of course!

- Is Rebecca going to be a main character or merely a secondary one? The answer to that probably lies in whether you decide to reprieve her death sentence by the end of the story. Readers don't like their heroes and heroines to die!
- Alternatively, if Rebecca dies before accomplishing her aim, perhaps it can be continued by her

daughter or some close friend who takes up the torch and becomes the protagonist of the story.

- How might this happen? Perhaps in going through Rebecca's papers after her death, this person finds clues to the trauma in her life.
- And what is that trauma that has filled Rebecca's life with such guilt? Has she betrayed someone? Done something that cost someone else's life? Defrauded a close friend? Covered up a murder?
- What will she do to try to make amends?

That is up to you!

CHAPTER *one*

It was one of those coincidences that are believable only in real life. A million-to-one chance. Heathrow in July, a myriad strangers crossing each other's paths as they make their way from one side of the globe to the other.

The eyes of the two women met for a mere split second as they rode the moving walkways in opposite directions. Over twenty years had passed, but each face retained enough of its youthful appearance to produce in the other a flash of startled recognition, a sudden racing of the heart beneath the designer jacket in one case and the crumpled T-shirt in the other, as the shock of memory and emotion hit home.

And then they were past each other. Swallowed up into the safety of the anonymous crowds. Two middle-aged women, one still slim and smart, the other's grip on youth lost too many hard years before.

Still shaken from that split-second confrontation

with her past, Sophie Drummond approached the Customs gates. The blood pounded in her ears and her legs in their high heels felt leaden as she stumbled off the walkway with her trolley of matching luggage. For a moment she tried to convince herself she had merely dreamed it. Surely that woman who had slipped by her so swiftly couldn't be Terri. It just wasn't possible.

But she had caught the swift doubletake of recognition, had seen her own fear reflected in that other startlingly aged face and knew she hadn't been mistaken.

It was an omen, Sophie shivered, a sign telling her that she should never have come.

But she'd had to. There'd been no choice about that. And she'd been sure that the risk after all this time would be minimal.

Only now did she realise how wrong she might have been.

Why it works

The very first sentence of this chapter should have grabbed our readers' attention immediately. References to a 'coincidence' and 'a million to one chance' will at once set them wondering what can be the import of this freak event.

In paragraph 2, we describe the meeting neither of our characters had dreamed possible. As well, we underline its significance by revealing that twenty years have passed since the two women last saw each other and that those two decades have treated them very differently. One is dressed in a designer jacket, which implies a well-to-do lifestyle, the other is wearing a crumpled T-shirt, implying the opposite. By referring to the 'shock of memory and emotion' we also imply that something that happened long ago has left a deep and painful mark on both of them.

In the paragraphs that follow we take up the story from the point of view of Sophie, whose affluence is made clear through her dress.

This opening is brief but intense, with plenty of potential. Let's see what we can come up with to extend the story.

- Who are Sophie and Terri? Are they related? Former friends or business colleagues?
- What happened to them, twenty years ago and since?
- Why did Sophie think it might be safe to come back 'after all this time'? Where has she been in the meantime?
- Why does this glimpse of Terri make her regret her decision?

- If Terri frightened too? Or is it Terri who arouses the fear in Sophie?
- If the latter, why?
- Are other people involved in whatever occurred?
- Perhaps Sophie and Terri were part of a group of teenagers who were caught up in something threatening or dangerous. Was it a youthful prank gone wrong? Did someone die? Perhaps it was a hit-and-run accident after all the group had been drinking. Or perhaps four young friends were on holiday together in a place like Bali and a drug-taking session ended in a death. Maybe someone else was falsely imprisoned.
- Most important, who is going to be your main character? How much does she know of what really happened?

Keep asking yourself those questions that prod your imagination and you'll see how your plotline can grow.

Chapter One

The call came through from Emergency Services at precisely 7.07 p.m.

Sergeant Tim Olson was the duty sergeant at the Bondi station that evening. He was 23 years old and to him the details meant nothing. As far as he was concerned it was just another Friday night homicide.

'So that's Unit 16, right? Second floor? Okay, we'll get a car there right away.'

Only after he passed on the information did the young sergeant discover that this was no ordinary murder.

For Colette Young, the night began with no inkling of what was to come. It was good to catch up with Andy again and she enjoyed the irony of an Englishman showing her around what had once been her home city. The restaurant they were eating in tonight hadn't existed when she'd left Sydney almost eighteen years ago. So much had changed. But not, unfortunately, the interest in Colette Young.

Now, as she followed Andy past the other diners towards the exit she could sense the curious glances even among this sophisticated clientele. No doubt, she thought wryly, they were trying to reconcile the newspaper photos of eighteen years ago with the person they saw now. Then, it had been wash-and-wear hair and serviceable jeans and T-shirts. Now it was an expensive sleek bob, the clinging, cashmere softness of a Jean Muir dress, and hand-made suede heels that lent a gratifying couple of extra inches to her petiteness.

The car was waiting, and Andy McRae grunted as they slipped into the back seat. 'Christ, I should never have had that dessert.' His accent was pure south London. 'This waistband's killing me. How come I never used to have problems with good old British stodge?'

'Come on, Andy,' Colette smiled. 'Who are you kidding? Long as I've known you you've been moaning about your weight.'

The bear-like Englishman looked at her and grinned. 'Stress, my love. Others drink or smoke, I eat.'

'The general consensus seems to be that exercise rather than Mars Bars is the way to go,' she teased. 'I thought after eighteen months here you'd be pounding the sands of Bondi every morning by now.'

Andy McRae groaned and patted his generous paunch.

'Get serious. My every waking moment is spent adding to your fortune, sweetheart.' He pulled a packet of Alka-Seltzer from his jacket pocket and popped one into his mouth. 'Still want to stop off at the office?'

It was a rhetorical question.

Andy McRae had been with her from the start, from that first takeover of a dying provincial newspaper chain to the magic moment when they'd entered the big league. By now, Andy could have afforded to take the easy path—a directorship with power and influence and none of the stresses of the daily grind. But Andy was a hands-on man, a newspaperman of the old school. As well as a friend and confidant.

In a spontaneous gesture, Colette patted the broad, plump hand that rested on the seat beside her.

'I'm very happy with the way things are going, Andy. You've done all I could have hoped for and more. Whatever the international successes might have meant, it was always important that I made it here.'

Their eyes met. Andy McRae knew exactly what she meant. He was one of the very few who knew what had happened to Colette Young. What made her run. Why she had taken on such impossible odds and dared to turn the tide. He respected her immensely. And loved her not much less.

As her cool fingers lifted from his own, the Englishman cursed himself for his crazy hope. He'd known Colette for more than a dozen years, yet, strong as the friendship was between them, there was still some invisible wall, an almost palpable reserve that he could never muster enough courage to breach.

Colette was a woman of many faces, as he had come to see. There was the hard-headed professional who drove herself relentlessly in the pursuit of her goals, the friend who would do anything for those she trusted and cared for, the witty, fun-loving raconteur who could light up the dullest of dinner parties.

Andy had seen the way other men had looked at her, seen the admiration and lust in their eyes. But if Colette had affairs, her discretion was complete. A natural reaction, he told himself, when your public profile was as high as hers. And after all they had achieved, there were plenty ready to plunge the knife—some as cruelly as possible, he knew.

Their driver was pulling up in front of the leased premises in East Sydney where Australia's newest daily was produced. With a grunt, Andy levered himself out of the rear seat. 'I won't be a moment,' he grinned over his shoulder.

Colette knew he was teasing. 'Yeah, I'll just hang around out here,' she replied as she slid out behind him.

For a moment she stood on the sidewalk and stared up at the sign that glowed above them. *The Flagship,* it read.

'I've still got to convince myself it's happening, Andy,' she said softly. She'd flown in only two days before. It was hard to believe she was now seeing her dream come true.

'It is, Col.' Andy McRae understood her mood as they climbed the steps to the main entrance. 'And the readership is growing every month,' he added as they were greeted by the uniformed security guard, who quickly moved to open the door. 'People want a choice. And a truly independent voice. That's the message we're getting loud and clear.'

Colette waited until they were inside the elevator before she said with quiet intensity, 'It's taken a long time, Andy, but it was the only way I knew to right a terrible wrong.'

Andy McRae knew exactly what she meant.

The night shift staff were busy at their desks, but none of them minded the interruption by the woman who was not only their boss but a legend. Most of them had leapt at the chance to join her team.

Colette greeted them all warmly before following Andy and the night editor to check the first edition of the next morning's newspaper. The headlines that day featured the resignation of a Cabinet minister over a funding scandal.

With a practised eye, she scanned the layout, made a few comments about details, then skimmed the next couple of pages.

And there it was. A small piece at the bottom of page 4. The victim's name jumped out at her, as familiar almost as her own.

As she stared at the spare, unemotional details, Colette felt the shock travel through her, leaving her weak-limbed, ashen-faced.

'Col...are you okay?'

Andy was frowning at her. Her change of expression must have been obvious.

Stiffly, she managed a nod. 'Yes, it's nothing...'

But Colette Young couldn't help wondering

what terrible thing she had done for God to keep making her pay for her sins over and over again.

Why it works

In the first section of this opening chapter we convey to readers that the victim was in the past a well-known figure simply by mentioning the duty sergeant's age and the fact that the victim's name means nothing to him, while implying, with 'this was no ordinary murder,' that to others it means a great deal.

Giving nothing more away at this intriguing point, we next introduce our heroine—and immediately sow the first hint of intrigue by referring to 'what was to come'. Readers should immediately be wondering how the murder is connected to the heroine.

We also reveal right away that Colette hasn't been back to Sydney, her home town, in almost eighteen years. Yet she is still of great interest to the public—a fact we convey by describing the reaction of the other diners. As always, the idea is to pose questions for our readers: What could Colette Young have done to attract media attention all those years ago? Why is she back in Sydney? She is clearly well-off. Was she always? What has she achieved in her time away?

We use the dialogue between Andy and Colette at this point to demonstrate the easy, close relationship between them and suggest that Andy has stronger feelings for Colette than friendship. We also tell our readers both what work they do and how they're connected: both are in the 'big league' of newspaper ownership.

After giving a little more information about our heroine's business, in paragraph 26 we reintroduce a hint of mystery by referring to the 'terrible wrong' that Colette has had to fight. Next we offer a brief glimpse of Colette functioning as 'boss' to indicate the sort of relationship she has with her employees. It is clearly a good one, as most have 'leapt at the chance' to work for the *Flagship*.

In paragraph 30 we neatly tie Colette's story into the incident that opened our chapter. Merely writing 'the victim's name jumped out at her' should be sufficient to indicate that she is reading about the murder. Consider how else we might have presented this information.

We might have written: 'Colette stared at the small article at the bottom of page four. A murder at Bondi had occurred earlier that evening. And suddenly the victim's name jumped out at her...' The difference is subtle, isn't it? But allowing readers to make some of the connections for themselves makes for a much more satisfying story.

As always, the chapter ends on a high note of intrigue that should leave our readers with plenty of questions:

- What has happened to Colette Young? What made her run?
- Why has she taken on such impossible odds and dared to turn the tide?
- What sin does Colette feel she is being made to pay for?
- What is her relationship with the murder victim, whose name is 'as familiar almost as her own'?
- How is the murder tied in to her present circumstances and her need to right a terrible wrong?

Our heroine's main goal is clear—to establish a newspaper empire. It is clear, too, that she is a driven woman. So other obvious questions to explore are:

- What has given her such drive and determination?
- Was her father the owner of a small metropolitan daily that was squeezed out of existence by an unscrupulous rival?
- Did the loss of his dream somehow cause his death?
- Is her main rival now the same man who was responsible for the demise of her father's business?

These would certainly be strong reasons to propel Colette towards her own goals.

- Is the murder victim a former lover of her rival? A woman who, when she found herself discarded, told Colette the truth about her lover's unscrupulous business practices?

Start asking those questions and see how quickly your storyline will grow.

Chapter One

The enemy smelled blood. The hunter was now the hunted. The newspaper headlines said it all as the scandal erupted from coast to coast. As ordinary citizens drank their morning coffee, they felt disillusioned and betrayed. For so long they had believed in Penny Rydge. Now it seemed that she was no different from all the rest.

In boardrooms, mansions, country clubs, many of the country's elite felt a sense of unbridled relief, of danger dispelled. Life could now go on as it had always been meant to. Penny Rydge had been muzzled at last.

For the victim of the outcry, the only sanctuary lay behind the triple-locked doors of her apartment. Eyes red from lack of sleep, Penny reached for the telephone that sat on the coffee table in front of her. In ten years she had made many enemies. The rich and powerful didn't forget. Now someone had been willing to risk all to shut her up.

She punched in the familiar number. When the secretary's voice answered she asked to speak to Steve Redmond.

'I'm sorry, Miss Rydge, Mr Redmond is not available to take calls.' From you...The unspoken coda was loud and clear.

Penny hung up without a word.

Dazed, she got to her feet and began to pace around the sparsely furnished living room. In six years she still hadn't found time to decorate properly. There had been so many more important things to do.

Pausing by the window, she inched back the drapes and looked down into the street. It was just a few minutes after seven, but already reporters who had once billed her as the country's most dangerous woman were clustered like hyenas around her front door.

Well, she didn't feel dangerous any longer. Just small and afraid and vulnerable. For if Steve didn't believe her, how could she begin to convince anyone else?

Fighting back despair, she turned away from the view of the street. None of this was random, of that she was sure. Somehow it was all tied in with Kirk Ostell.

And that was why nothing was going to make her give up.

Why it works

This chapter starts with a couple of very provocative sentences, the sort that demand the reader's attention. Adding to their impact are references to 'scandal' and ordinary people 'disillusioned' and 'betrayed'. By the end of the first paragraph we have told the reader that our heroine has somehow failed and let these people down. And in paragraph 2 we reveal that her failure is being celebrated by the rich and powerful.

Without offering any more detail about what she might have done, we next show our heroine under siege and convey her belief that one of the wealthy enemies she's made over the last decade has plotted against her.

In paragraph 4 we raise the stakes by indirectly showing the one person she turns to for help refusing to take her call. At the same time, we raise some interesting questions in our readers' minds about the identity of Steve Redmond. Who is he? How might he have been able to help? Is he perhaps an ex-lover?

In paragraph 7 we underline Penny's commitment to her career of helping or championing ordinary people by letting on that even after six years Penny hasn't had time to finish decorating her apartment. This is a much subtler way of giving readers information about a character than saying 'Penny was consumed by her work doing x.' The message is nonetheless clear: Penny Rydge is a woman of action, whose idealism dominates her life. And, despite her traumatic circumstances, she is not going to give up. This lays the groundwork for conflict in the story. We tell the reader that the action is propelled by our character's fight to clear her name and bring to justice those responsible for her downfall.

By the end of the chapter the reader's head should be buzzing with questions—as should yours.

- Why is Penny known as the country's 'most dangerous woman'?
- Why is she under siege by reporters?
- Who is Kirk Ostell, and what has he done to cause her such trouble?
- How will she restore her good name?

Over to you!

Chapter One

Even three years later, there were occasions when she still saw recognition in some stranger's face. The frown of memory from a passerby in the street, the quick glance of a fellow passenger on a plane. Occasionally those bolder or more curious than others would actually approach her and ask, 'Aren't you—?'

Angela Ryan would give a quick, unsmiling nod, doing her best to discourage the interest of these intrusive strangers. She didn't belong to them any longer. Those days were over. They had lasted close to a decade. And when everything had changed she had closed the door on them all.

She had done her best to forget, but when memory, unbidden, forced its way through the barricades of time, it seemed as if it had been someone else living that life. Someone who had been totally alive, who had lived every day to the hilt. Despite the danger. Or maybe because of it.

But all that had changed on that October day

three years ago. Guts, determination, stamina, courage—everything she had always counted on had let her down. Like glass in a furnace, her world had melted around her, leaving her numb, adrift. As if the person she had been had disappeared.

Her name was still Angela Ryan, but she felt as if it belonged to a stranger, not to the person she had been for 37 years.

Afterwards, there had been the funeral in the sixteenth-century church in Cambridgeshire. The mourners had given her their sympathy, even though her status had never been formalised. She had been with Simon almost five years though, and Peter and Louise Colbert, genteel, reserved, had done their best to acknowledge that her loss would bite every bit as deeply as their own. She had been so grateful that Simon's parents had been understanding enough to embrace and comfort her in her sorrow.

It had been hard to leave that refined, middle-class home. Being there, with his parents, had made her feel she still had something left of the man she had loved. But some sort of rationality had ultimately told her she could no longer intrude on the Colbert's well-concealed devastation.

For three months afterwards she had stayed in London, at the unoccupied Pimlico flat of a colleague, unable to make any decision about her future. How could she do that when she was barely capable of opening her eyes each morning, of facing the suffocating endlessness of another day?

Zombie-like, she would dress in whatever was to hand and, face bare and hair uncared for, spend her days walking the winter-gloomy streets of the city. Blind to everyone and everything around her, she would eat only when reminded by the pain in her belly, stopping in some nondescript cafe for a sandwich she couldn't finish and a cup of coffee that grew cold as she sat transfixed by memory.

In the late evening, when she hoped enough time had passed to allow her to reach again for some artificial inducement to sleep, she would find her way back to the empty, anonymous flat.

But pills and alcohol couldn't stop the dreams. And in them she was with him again, breathing the scent of his skin, stroking his face, running her fingers through his springy, dark hair and feeling the sensual weight of his hard body against her own.

Often she would jolt awake and, lying in the darkness, would listen to the throb and hum of the city and the awful sound of her own tears.

In the end it was Jeannie who came and got

her. She was one of the few who had kept in touch. One of the very few Angela Ryan hadn't used or let down.

And Jeannie had taken her home.

'Christ, Angie...I've only had a couple of hours' sleep in three bloody days!'

Through bleary, bloodshot eyes the cameraman blinked awake to see Angela Ryan's face staring down into his own. At almost the same moment he realised that the pain he could feel in his ribs was being caused by the tip of his tormentor's thick, leather boot.

'Wakey, wakey, Ray. We didn't come here to sleep through the bloody revolution. Grab that camera and move it. Lee's already downstairs.'

Grumbling and swearing under his breath, Ray Jensen struggled out of the covers and in the weak light from the solitary unshaded bulb felt for his fur-lined boots under the bed. He was still wearing the clothes he'd gone to sleep in a short time before, and his fleshy face was shadowed by a thick stubble.

'I'd give my right ball for a coffee,' he groaned again as he heaved his heavy equipment onto his shoulders and followed the impatient journalist out of the hotel room. They were on the eleventh floor and were forced to enter the icy, malodorous darkness of the stairwell to make their way to ground level. The elevator had stopped working ten days ago and no one had bothered to fix it. But by now they'd all spent enough time in the Soviet capital to know that was par for the course.

'Talk to me nicely and I might save your sex life.' Torch in hand, Angela was clattering down the steep stairs ahead of him. 'I've still got 500 grams of pure Arabia left. Soon as this is in the can I'll give you enough for a cup.' Her voice echoed in the confined space.

'Hey, anyone ever tell you you're all heart, Ange?'

They were nearing street level and through the thick concrete walls they could hear the swelling noise outside.

Angela grinned in the dim light. 'No one—and if they did I'd think I was getting soft.'

Ray Jensen was sure she wasn't joking. By 6 a.m. the crowd in Red Square had swelled to an estimated half a million. Film and television crews from around the globe were jockeying for the best vantage points as they filmed the death throes of the once mighty Soviet Union.

Surrounded by the chanting, heaving crowds, Angie began arguing loudly with a French camera crew who were trying to move her on so they could place their own presenter in the prime location she had assumed.

But Angela Ryan had had plenty of practice in standing her ground. Her French was limited, but fortunately consisted mostly of insults, and with black looks and plentiful swearing protests the French were forced to move on.

'Okay, Ray, let's go.' As her sound technician adjusted his controls, Angie reached into the pocket of her green, fur-lined anorak and pulled out a comb which she ran quickly through her thick, dark brown hair. It was her only concession to grooming for on-air presentation.

Ray held up two fingers and Angie took the proffered microphone. In a moment the camera was rolling.

'Over the last six hours the situation here in Red Square has grown more tense. Estimates now put the crowd at close to half a million but no one is yet sure if the authorities are poised to react...'

It was a three-minute grab, shot direct by satellite to a worldwide audience of millions. Most would be barely able to believe what they were seeing. But English-speaking viewers would be reassured to find Angela Ryan once again in the thick of the action. The slightly built brunette was a familiar sight wherever in the world a hot spot caught fire. Casually dressed, face bereft of make-up, the 34-year-old foreign correspondent had filed a long list of tough stories. Those who worked with her sometimes felt driven beyond the limits of personal safety, but the male ego ensured there was never any official complaint. If Angela Ryan could handle it, so could they.

Why it works

Again we hit our readers' intrigue buttons in the opening sentence. Here is a character who is still recognised by strangers 'even three years later'. The implication is that she once had a very high profile. Readers should instantly start wondering what gave Angela Ryan such wide recognition, and what has happened to remove her from the public eye?

In paragraph 2 we show that Angela does not relish the attention of these 'intrusive strangers', and feels she is no longer public property. Again, we let the questions dangle a bit here. Was she an actress? a politician? a media personality? an undercover agent? You'll have learned by now, I hope, that it's by denying readers immediate answers that you best keep their interest.

In paragraph 3 we continue our teasing, offering just enough information to add to the mystery. Next, we give a picture of our heroine from her own perspective. She sees herself as a woman with 'guts, determination, stamina and courage'. But three years ago something happened that has obviously had an immense impact on her life.

The mention of the funeral in paragraph 6 begins to give some clue to the traumatic incident that has affected her so badly. But again the information is subtly given. Instead of baldly stating that Angela was the dead man's lover, we refer to the fact that 'her status had never been formalised'. We also mention that they were together for five years and that their partnership was strong enough for Angela to be accepted by Simon's parents. Throughout these paragraphs we make it clear how much in love she was with him and how much his loss has affected her. Yet not once do we baldly state: 'Angela was madly in love with Simon and his death plunged her into anguish'. By now you should have seen that conveying information in this way makes the reader participate more actively in the story and identify much more closely with your characters.

We have used a flashback here to tell about the death of Angela's lover. In the same way we describe the aftermath—how our heroine stayed at a colleague's flat in London (the implication being that she wasn't a resident of the city), how she wandered 'zombie-like' around the streets, 'transfixed by memory'. Notice how we get a lot more impact and immediacy by *showing* our character's emotional state rather than *telling* about it. Nowhere do we say: 'Angela was distraught over the loss of the man she loved.' Instead we follow her through her bleak days, not caring how she looks, unable to eat, dependent on drugs and alcohol.

And in the second last paragraph we surprise the reader with the information that Angela had only one friend—Jeannie—and that she was 'one of the very few Angela Ryan hadn't used or let down.' This sentence should have our readers biting their nails with curiosity. Heroines aren't supposed to use their friends or let them down. The fact that Angela does, helps make her a more interesting character. But you will later have to develop a profile for her that will offer some excuse for her behaviour and thus restore her 'heroine' status.

- Perhaps it's her 'dangerous' job that pushes Angela to extremes and makes it hard for her to maintain stable relationships? What could that job be?
- Did Simon work in the same field?
- How did they meet? Did they like each other from their first meeting?
- Why does Jeannie stand by Angela? Does she owe her a favour, or does she see to the heart of her friend?
- The action starts three years after the funeral, so

> what is Angela doing now? I think allowing a reasonably long time span is important, as it will enable Angela to become credibly involved in another love relationship, one that might heal the pain left by Simon's loss.

As with all the other Chapter Ones offered here, it is your job now to decide on the heroine's goal and who or what is opposing her.

Chapter One

She had waited until the service was under way before slipping in at the side door of the church.

The rear pews were empty and she slid onto the polished wood, a petite, fine-featured woman wearing an elegantly simple black dress, her copper hair drawn back in a gold clasp. As she took her seat, a couple of curious heads turned, then looked away.

Kate Lyle didn't really expect to be recognised. At 38 she was a long way from the jeans-clad nineteen-year-old whose hair had hung in a thick curtain to her waist.

The number of mourners in the inner-city Anglican church surprised her. But then, Kate reminded herself, Bernie Lang had always been popular. At least with those who shared his belief in the rights and freedoms of their fellow men.

From behind her dark glasses she scrutinised the rows of heads. An impossible task to pick out anyone she might know. It was so long ago.

CHAPTER ONE

Everyone and everything had changed. On the way in from the airport the day before, she'd been amazed by the differences that twenty years had wrought. The choking traffic and crowded streets, the forests of high-rise apartments, the sense of bustle and energy. It was almost like being back in London, she'd thought. Except for the sun.

Now, shifting her head a little to the left, Kate could just see the woman in the front row. Nancy...It had to be. The curls were the same, although a different, lighter colour. She was flanked by two young girls, and had a comforting arm curled around one of them. Bernie Logan's widow and daughters.

Kate wondered how it felt to be a widow at just 39. Then a glimmer of bitterness lit her hazel eyes. Maybe not that much different from being a divorcee. Pain and loss. A life needing to be re-shaped, pointed in a new direction. Exactly what she had faced just five years ago. Only there hadn't been any children, thank God. The prospect of motherhood had seemed unbearable. After what had happened.

Abruptly, she brought her attention back to the ritual. The minister was calling on one of the mourners to step forward and deliver the eulogy.

A man, blond, very tall, rose to his feet

somewhere near the front and with quick, easy grace made his way to the pulpit.

Kate frowned. There was something strangely familiar about that walk. Then, as he turned to face the congregation, she saw the aquiline nose, the confident set of the mouth and chin, the serious green eyes.

And her face paled with shock.

Why it works

Yet another funeral...We give no clue at the start who's died or why, but the church setting gives our heroine a chance to look about her and reminisce while the ritual unfolds. And it gives us the space to do quite a lot of exposition while we carefully build our readers' interest.

In paragraphs 2 and 3 we contrast the present Kate Lyle with her younger self. And in paragraph 4 we reveal that the service is for Bernie Lang, and make clear that he was a well-regarded man, a man with a social conscience. We also imply that Kate had known or been associated with him in her youth. Now we tell our readers that our character has been out of the country a long time, living in London. By shifting Kate's gaze to Bernie Lang's widow, we show that she knew Nancy too. Then, by following Kate's thoughts, we sketch in some more background. She has been divorced for five years—and sees parallels between her own situation and the grief of Nancy Lang. The allusion to 'bitterness' should alert readers to the fact that the divorce was not an amicable one. We also slip in the fact (which our readers will need to know later) that Kate, unlike Nancy, didn't have children and is thankful for the fact. At this point we don't explain why—that would spoil the suspense. Instead, we actually build suspense by alluding to 'what had happened'.

We end the chapter by introducing—albeit briefly—a new character, and a further hint of mystery. Our readers will not be able to help reading on now.

And when they do, you will have to have a parcel of answers ready for them:

- Who was Bernie Lang?
- What caused his death?
- What sort of work did he do to live out his social concerns?
- Why has Kate come all the way from London to his funeral?
- Why was her marriage not a success?
- What happened that made her thankful that she didn't have children?
- Who is the man who is going to read the eulogy to Bernie Lang? Is he an ex-lover? A former

business rival? A married man with whom she had an affair?

- Why is Kate affected by his presence?
- What mission will Kate set out to accomplish now that she's back in Australia?
- Will she be welcomed by Nancy Lang or cursed for having pushed Bernie beyond reasonable limits in some way?
- Does the allusion to jeans and waist-length hair imply that Kate was once a student activist? Was she so reviled all those years ago that she was forced to leave Australia?
- What has she accomplished since?
- Is she taking a risk coming back at this time?
- What was her relationship with the dead man?

Look for answers to those myriad questions and you might just find yourself with a plot.

CHAPTER ONE

It was the last call of the evening. And almost at once the voice triggered some vague memory. Probably someone she had spoken to before, Suzette told herself as she sat behind the microphone in the dim light of the glass-walled studio.

People often seemed lonelier on Sunday nights. They needed someone to talk to. And between 9 and 10 p.m. it was Suzette Baker who was there at the other end of the line, taking the cries of help from those who found the pressures of modern life too much to bear. Tonight, as usual, the switchboard for Heart to Heart had run hot with the usual array of problems: rape, incest, drugs, domestic violence, sexual dysfunction, postnatal blues...And in her quiet, soothing voice, therapist Suzette Baker did her best to offer comfort and advice.

Whenever she wondered just how much good she could really do in the short time allotted to each caller, she comforted herself with the thought that perhaps merely having mustered the courage to take that first step might help her callers go further and seek professional help face to face. Despite its inadequacies, Heart to Heart fulfilled a need, Suzette knew.

Pencil in hand, she listened carefully now to the voice at the other end of the line. A woman's voice. And again it struck a faint chord of memory.

'It—it happened eight weeks ago…' The woman spoke falteringly. 'And I still can't come to terms with the shock.' She sounded close to tears.

'Tell me about it,' Suzette coaxed gently.

'I—my husband was killed. His car ran off the road. They found his body in the river…'

Suzette could hear the sharp intake of breath as her caller struggled for control. 'Are you alone?' she asked soothingly. 'Do you have friends or family who can help you through this bad time?'

'There are things I can't tell my family…I'm afraid. It's just strange that—' Abruptly, the woman broke off.

'What do you mean…strange?' Suzette encouraged.

There was a long silence during which all Suzette could hear was the sound of the woman's heavy breathing. It was those silences, or a caller's breaking down in tears, that she found difficult to handle on live radio.

'Please,' she urged sympathetically, 'let me help you.'

And finally it came out in a rush.

'I'm not convinced it was an accident!' Now there was a panicky edge to the woman's voice. 'I think my husband was murdered. And I think I know why. Only I don't know where to go, who I can trust. That's why I'm calling you! I'm afraid—'

With a sharp click the line went dead.

Disconcerted as she was, as she wound up the program Suzette did her best to be upbeat, to smooth the moment over and leave her listeners on a more positive note.

Yet she was frowning as she took off her headphones. Somewhere, sometime recently, she knew she had heard that caller's voice before.

Why it works

While this opening might appear simple, it wasn't easy to write, mainly because we had to include two essential points. First, we had to establish that the heroine is in a radio studio, and then we had to get across a sense of mystery and intrigue. We could have begun by writing something like this: 'It was Sunday evening and Suzette sat behind the control panel of her local radio station facing her usual line-up of calls.'

The reason we didn't do that is that it would have delayed the hint of mystery that makes readers sit up and take notice. As I've said more than once, the main thing to keep in mind when you're writing a beginning for any story is the reader's attention—the elusive fish that you must hook at the first bite. Remember that there are hundreds and hundreds of other writers' novels out there on bookstore shelves, so you've got to do all you possibly can to make the browser buy yours!

A key aspect of the rest of this chapter is the effective and subtle way in which we've handled the exposition. By paragraph 3 we have conveyed to readers what Suzette Baker does, the name of her program and its schedule. But other than our mention of her 'quiet, soothing voice', we have not yet given a physical description of our heroine. Pausing to do that now would distract readers from the essentials of the story.

As soon as we've given the necessary information we jump right back into the mystery. Again we use dialogue to relate it—this time between our heroine and her caller. This is a more filmic way of doing things, and gives us the chance to draw out and give out the intriguing details gradually.

We also use the dialogue to build Suzette's character, showing her gentleness in drawing her caller out. If we'd shown her glancing at the clock or stifling a yawn, we'd have given a very different picture of her. Every word in this vital opening section of your novel should count towards building plot, suspense and character in a subtle, gradual way. The skill lies in doing that without being heavy-handed.

As you analyse this opening chapter, pay close attention to how the sense of mystery is conveyed: Suzette has a vague memory of having heard her caller's voice before, the woman is frightened and reveals the fact that she suspects her husband's death was murder, the line suddenly goes dead. And we leave readers with so many unanswered questions! Again, it's your turn to find the answers.

- Who is the caller?
- Why does she suspect her husband was murdered?
- Who has cut off the call?
- Does the woman have an accent Suzette recognises? Could she be the wife of a foreign diplomat who is mixed up in some underhand business? Or perhaps she is the wife of a policeman who has been intent on following up on some particular case despite being overruled by his superiors.

- Where has Suzette heard the voice before? Has she met the woman socially? Was she a former client? And who, if anyone, has overheard her conversation? Her son, who doesn't want his mother's life put in danger too? Someone more sinister? Or was the woman merely too frightened to go on?
- What will Suzette do next? Will she remember where she heard the voice?
- Will the woman make contact again—perhaps this time by letter, or by making an appointment to see Suzette in her rooms?

Taking your cue from these questions, try to build your story—and, at the same time, flesh out your characters and their dilemmas.

Part 3

Expanding your opening chapter into a finished storyline

I thought it might be helpful to analyse one of my complete works to give you further insight into the way beginnings fuse with middles and endings. The following story was included in an anthology of short stories and was also published in *The Australian Women's Weekly*. I prefer to think of it as a story about love than as a 'romance'. Appropriately in this instance, it also deals with the themes of writing and creativity.

Unlike a novel, a short story usually has no subplots. But it still needs to provide motivation and conflict for the heroine or, as in this case, the hero.

As you read this story, try to identify where the turning points come—those incidents that give the story extra momentum.

The Gift

Harry Benson was a success. If by success one means the possession of wealth, fame, freedom, acclaim. For most of us that's usually enough. For Harry Benson at 51 it seemed enough too. There were the homes in Sydney, London, the south of France. The regular sojourns in Martinique, New England or Chamonix. The burgundy Bentley and the pewter-coloured Porsche. The legendary wine cellar.

Harry was the sort of man invariably described by the press as 'dapper' and 'fastidious', with his monogrammed shirts from Turnbull and Asser and his footwear from New and Lingwood, Jermyn Street. His tailors outfitted dukes and princes, though he still liked to confound with the occasional splash of continental motley from Basile of Rome.

The world, as they say, was Harry Benson's oyster. He'd come a long way from the shy country lad who'd been seventeen before he had even set foot in Pitt Street, Sydney.

He might never have got that far if it hadn't been for Mrs Daley. Her sharp, experienced eyes had seen the potential from an early age and she had done all she could to encourage it. It was under Mrs Daley's forceful tutelage that Harry had blossomed. It was she who had made the young boy believe there might be more ahead of him than leaving school at fifteen and landing an apprenticeship at Hadley's garage.

Sometimes, even now, Harry would wake in the middle of the night amid the sweaty tangle of his designer sheets having dreamt he was doing exactly that; covered in grease, head stuck inside some recalcitrant machine, while the smeared pages of some girlie wall calendar fluttered past the years.

Thank God, he would murmur aloud in the darkness. Thank God for Mrs Daley. He had taken her advice, had ignored the teasing of his peers, soothed the anxieties of his widowed mother who had been looking forward to another pay cheque, and applied himself assiduously to his studies.

The scholarship to Sydney University had made it all worthwhile. He remembered the pride mixed with sad tears in his mother's tired eyes as she had waved him off on the train to the Big Smoke.

'Write to me, Harry, darling! Don't forget to write!

Write! He smiled even now when he remembered his mother's words.

How seldom life goes to plan. Accountancy. A career. Safe and secure. Then marriage, a home of his own, children. That was how it was meant to be.

And look what had happened.

Not that Harry was complaining. His success had come unexpectedly, though not without sacrifice. Or should he call it suffering?

The first shock had been his absolute loathing of his chosen academic path. The mistake, he saw, was to have been so focused on the end result. The name plaque on the office door, the gleaming desk, the suits and respect.

Only a sense of duty to Mrs Daley and his mother had kept him going. His head had ached through indescribably tedious lectures. His soul revolted as he wasted hours on another unfathomable assignment. Balance sheets and rows of figures did not make Harry's blood burn with passion.

But women did. Maybe it was his edge of country shyness, the respect and good manners bred in him by his mother and Mrs Daley for the opposite sex in general, but Harry found himself a hit. Girls liked him. Girls liked him!

And if at first he was too reticent to make a move, that didn't hinder the fairer sex. As he listened wide-eyed to their compliments, Harry realised for the first time the appeal of his dark, silky hair, his clear, green eyes and his unblemished skin.

And then he got the hang of it. He learned to

kiss, to breathe warmly around small ears, to whisper sweetly, to cuddle and stroke.

Yet quite instinctively Harry possessed the most important attribute of all. He listened. He was genuinely interested in what women had to say. And the more he listened the more he came to understand these scented, emotional creatures.

It was a knowledge that allowed Harry to far outstrip his peers. By listening, he discovered what women wanted in bed as well as out. Harry became a lover *par excellence*. He achieved that hair-trigger balance so rare in the male—becoming as tender and gentle as he was forceful and demanding.

Young, enthusiastic, energetic, Harry would have been a fool not to take full advantage of his position. And as lover succeeded lover, each parting was handled with a sensitivity and gentleness that left no ill-feeling in its wake. Discretion and diplomacy were his tools of trade.

Thanks mainly to the pleasures of his love life, Harry managed to endure the labour of his studies. Graduating with an eminently respectable degree, he landed the first position he applied for. Links and Doherty, long established in the city, had expanded to the North Shore. A bright, young graduate like Harry Benson would fit in very well.

But the receipt of a regular pay packet did not make Harry less antipathetic to his chosen career. From 8.30 until 5.03 he fought back panic and resentment in his cheerless cupboard as he struggled with the debits and credits of various faceless merchants. Only his allotted 40 minutes for lunch allowed a temporary escape.

As he joined the lunchtime queues in the local sandwich shop, despair ate at him. How was he going to stand it for the rest of his life? But what would he do if he left? He was too old now to land any sort of apprenticeship. And what of his mother and Mrs Daley? How could he let them down, disappoint their expectations?

So engrossed was Harry in his painful musings that for the first time he found no solace in the opposite sex. As he sat with his packet of mixed sandwiches in the local park, the tanned bare legs and sideways smiles of the secretaries and shop girls were lost on him.

Then, one lunchtime, three months after the start of his enslavement by Links and Doherty, he sought refuge from a sudden summer storm in the hallowed peacefulness of the local library.

And that's when it happened. The meeting that changed Harry's life.

In all the television, radio and press interviews handled so deftly in the years that followed, Harry never once mentioned her name. But it was clear to all that there had been *someone*. Someone important. The catalyst. Someone who had made Harry Benson the success he was.

It was the aftermath of that meeting and what it wrought in Harry's life that had set him on the path to wealth and fame, the path that made him a household name. He took the first tentative steps the day he posted the manila envelope—yes, lifted from the stationery files of Links and Doherty—with the eight pages defiantly written during working hours.

Three weeks later the telephone call came. It was the features editor of the *Australian Women's Weekly*, congratulating Harry on his success. Of over 400 entries, it was Harry Benson's that had been chosen to be published in the following edition.

'I must admit it was a bit of a surprise—finding out you're a man, I mean,' the editor was saying. 'H. Benson. Well, to tell you the truth, all of us here just assumed that only a woman could understand other women like that. A truly wonderful story, Mr Benson—such feeling, such sensitivity!'

These words were repeated in Harry's ear just five days after the appearance his story *From the*

Heart. The caller this time was Eleanor Martin, an editor at a major publishing house.

'It was so *sensitive*, so full of *feeling*, Mr Benson. I just had to get in touch. Have you written anything else? Everyone who's read this has been so moved, so completely overwhelmed by the strength of the emotion. They can hardly believe a man wrote it. You, uh, did write it yourself, didn't you, Mr Benson?'

Later, Eleanor Martin would look back on her impulsive phone call and wonder at the convulsions of fate. For not only was Harry Benson indeed the author, he also had a completed novel in his possession! The editor's voice held a squeak of excitement. 'I think we should meet, Mr Benson. Are you free for lunch sometime this week? And perhaps you would be so kind as to bring the manuscript with you.'

Eleanor Martin was 56, divorced, and her interest in the opposite sex had died many years before. But after just ten minutes in Harry Benson's company she felt her juices heating like a kettle coming to the boil. Those wonderful eyes, so intense and direct, those slim, sensual hands, that diffident charm and the perfect manners. If this long work was as good as the story...

That night, after finishing the manuscript hours after midnight, Eleanor Martin had her first erotic dream for a decade. Inflamed by Harry's prose, his powerful tale of love, passion and loss, she writhed fitfully in her single bed and woke with a smile on her flushed, tired face.

Whatever happened, she had to have Harry Benson. If only in her dreams as a lover, then certainly in real life as one of her authors. In the pragmatic light of day Eleanor Martin knew that if this bright, handsome talent could have such an impact on her, the reaction from younger women readers would be beyond doubt.

Once her employers read the manuscript themselves they needed little persuasion to launch their editor's find with a trumpet blast of publicity. And their faith in their discovery was not misplaced. The reviews for *A Certain Desire* were overwhelming in their praise.

'Hard to believe the writer is male...Harry Benson shows he understands the deepest corners of a woman's soul.'

'Benson's writing reveals a man unafraid to share his suffering for love.'

And from one of the more popular women's magazines: 'Harry Benson—where can we find more like you?'

The fact that reviews by critics of his own sex were unanimous in their scorn did not cause Harry, his publishers, or his female fans a moment's loss of sleep. Harry's writing spoke to women. It was only natural that men without Harry's insight and sensitivity, lacking Harry's courage to reveal their fears and suffering, would be made to feel uncomfortable.

Such an avalanche of positive publicity buried the few odd carpings and ensured that first-run copies of *A Certain Desire* sold out in record time. With second and third print runs also disappearing as fast as they hit the stores, Harry Benson made Australian publishing history. And for the stunned and rather dazed author, it didn't stop there.

For the first time the publisher's English parent company, unable to ignore the lure of sure-fire profits, was forced to accommodate an antipodean author in its domestic publishing schedules. It even went so far as to bring Harry to the old country for unprecedented press exposure.

Within a week of its release in the United Kingdom, *A Certain Desire* shot to first place on the fiction best-seller list. British women, too, it seemed, found the tale of a hero baring his soul as irresistible as their Australian counterparts had. And they were just as eager to catch a glimpse of a man who wasn't afraid to write from the depths of his heart. Wherever Harry was scheduled to appear, he was mobbed by adoring, bright-eyed fans, who were further captivated by the author's charm and good looks. Amid all the hubbub of publisher's cocktail parties, press interviews and book signings, Harry Benson could hardly believe what was happening to him.

He had been back in Australia only three days when news arrived of further success. Not that it came as any surprise to Eleanor Martin or his ecstatic publishers. Wasn't it inevitable that such a valuable property would become the subject of a bidding war between rival film producers?

The triumphant editor could hardly contain her excitement as, champagne in hand, she rang the bell at Harry's recently acquired Double Bay home to break the good news in person.

'You're a sensation, Harry!' The same squeak of excitement was in Eleanor Martin's voice as she followed her star author into his sunny living room. The packing cases were evidence of his recent occupancy. 'They're talking Peter O'Toole or Richard Burton to play the lead! This is the big time, darling!'

The endearment slipped out. Eleanor couldn't help it. Just as in the heat of the moment, she couldn't help giving in to an impulse she had dreamed of so often: she kissed Harry Benson on the cheek. Until that second Eleanor had been contemptuous of terms like 'swoon'. Swooning was something silly teenagers were prone to, not mature, sophisticated career women like herself. But the whiff of Harry Benson's aftershave, the accidental caress of his soft, dark hair, the sensation of his cool, firm skin beneath her lips—for one reverberating moment Eleanor felt herself transformed into a pure sensation.

The object of her malaise, thank God, didn't seem to notice. Fighting to gather her composure, the taste of young male flesh still burning her lips, she said, 'Harry…' Something had happened to her voice. She tried again. 'Harry, you've got to write another book. You can do it, can't you?'

Harry Benson didn't answer. He crossed the room to one of the packing cases and pulled open the cardboard flaps. With an expression of shy modesty he produced a manila folder. 'I've started, Eleanor. It's called *One Day at a Time*.'

Eleanor Martin felt her breathing grow shallow. A professional reaction this time, thank the Lord.

'Is…is it…you didn't try to do anything different, did you Harry? The suffering and pain—they're still there?'

Harry Benson directed his green gaze outside the large picture window. Yet he didn't really see the expensive view.

'My hero's still paying the price,' he softly assured his tremulous editor.

Only Harry knew exactly the price he had paid for his harbour view. Over the next three decades he grew rich on his talent for writing the sorts of novels women couldn't get enough of. His wealth brought him freedom, allowed him to establish homes abroad, and made him the object of envy of those more stylised, less literal writers who gathered awards in place of stocks and shares.

Oh, there were a few who sought to emulate his success. But none succeeded. There was something about the 'voice' in Harry's work. The emotions rang so true. There was an honesty in his portrayal of a series of similar heroes, all suffering for love, that told women Harry Benson was writing from the heart.

As he grew older, Harry—as can happen with men—also grew more attractive. By his late 40s his dark hair was elegantly threaded with silver, though still as thick as ever. His complexion, saved from the sun by his indoor occupation, remained youthful and firm. And while he could afford the best of restaurants, he ate sparely and avoided the spreading flesh of middle age.

Harry's fame, his attractiveness and charm and, let's be honest, his abundant wealth made him a target for adoring women everywhere. When, as inevitably happened in his numerous chat-show appearances, the subject of his continuing bachelorhood came up, Harry, by subtle glances, fidgets, soft sighs, managed to convey that while he loved women generally and unreservedly—no breath of scandal or ambiguity there—his one regret was that life hadn't worked out for him in matters of the heart. 'Perhaps,' he would sometimes add, 'that's why I'm so obsessed with writing about love.' Usually he would then lift his shoulders ever so slightly, as if in resigned dismissal of his misfortune. 'Maybe I'm trying to will it into my life.'

An avalanche of fan mail was the invariable aftermath of such an admission. Women of all ages and backgrounds were only too keen to help their favourite author in his search for personal fulfilment.

But Harry walked a very careful path through the thicket of his opportunities. He enjoyed female company and would happily have affairs, but only with the sort of women he felt would make no demands. Strong, independent career women with lives of their own invariably suited him best.

On occasion, however, his charm, his style, his skill and consideration as a lover proved too much for even the most seemingly self-sufficient of women. But Harry was quick to read the signs. As soon as he sensed a lover's desire for true intimacy he would extricate himself from the relationship without delay. It was the only way.

Life might have continued on this quite acceptable path if not for what occurred one April morning in the year Harry turned 51.

On yet another promotional tour for his latest book, *Tomorrow Is the Same,* his publicists were hurrying him through the foyer of an inner-city hotel. Outside, in the sunshine, a limousine was waiting to deliver Harry to the next interview.

A woman crossed the hotel foyer and Harry turned to look at her. Their eyes met—and locked. It seemed to Harry as if his heart had suddenly swelled to fill his chest. His breath was choking him and his knees felt like foam rubber. As his escorts swept past, Harry stopped dead.

'Marie!'

'Harry.' She gave him a dazed smile. 'How...how are you?'

'Fine...just fine...'

It was the sort of dialogue Harry would have scorned in his own carefully engineered sentences. But he was capable of nothing else as he stared at the slim, well-dressed woman with her pale, upswept hair and warm, dark eyes.

'What a surprise! Are you promoting a new book?' Her aplomb was greater than his. But that might have been expected.

'Yes...it's...' But Harry didn't want to talk about the career that had sustained him all those years in between. 'Do you live in Sydney?'

His minders were throwing him impatient frowns, muttering about schedules and traffic.

'Yes, in Roseville. I'm—'

Harry interrupted. Time was against him. Again. 'Is your marriage...' *God*, he was about to blurt it out, was going to ask if she was happy. And it mattered. It really mattered!

She blinked and said softly, 'Actually I'm a widow now. Derek died three years ago.'

'Mr Benson,' a firm hand on his arm, 'we're going to need every minute.'

'Yes...yes...' Harry fumbled in his wallet, the etched pigskin one he'd bought on the Via Loggetta in Florence a couple of years before. 'Please.' He thrust his card at her. 'Call me. Maybe...Maybe you might let me take you to dinner.'

There was no time to read her expression before he was swept away.

The interviewer irritated him. For the first time Harry wondered why he bothered. His books never failed to sell in their millions. Why was he wasting his time with this sleek, fatuous name dropper whose smile disappeared with the camera light?

But despite his emotional turmoil Harry managed his usual professional exchange, as he did during the rest of the day. The questions never varied. All he had to remember was the title of his latest offering, though even that was difficult after the shock he had just experienced.

It was only when he was back in the blessed solitude of his own home, glass of scotch in hand, that he could begin to digest the emotions engendered by the morning's unexpected meeting.

Marie Gordon. *Marie Gordon...*

He knew exactly when he had seen her last. Twenty-nine years ago. She had been nineteen, three years younger than himself. He had never forgotten. Any of it. He took a long swallow of his drink and wondered if she might even call that evening. Confident of his appeal and celebrity, Harry was certain she would get in touch.

It was only when three days had passed without any contact that his confidence began to ebb. Suddenly he felt as vulnerable and exposed as he had all those years before. And slowly, relentlessly, panic scraped away the scab of deeper memory.

He had met Marie Gordon on that rainy

afternoon when he had sought shelter in the library close to the offices of Links and Doherty.

He was edging past her in the narrow aisle between Reference and A, a slim, fair-haired girl dressed in a plain skirt and sweater, attempting to extract a large reference book from the upper shelf.

'Need a hand?'

She turned, surprised, and Harry caught sight of her face for the first time. Pale, perfect skin, luminous, dark eyes ringed with mink-thick lashes, a wide, sensual mouth that was lifting in a grateful smile.

'Thanks. It'd be a help.'

Harry reached up. 'This one? The book on Sydney?'

'Yes, thanks.'

He pulled it out and saw it was a guide to the city. She took it from his hands. 'Thanks a lot. I need to take some notes.'

'You're not a local?'

'Oh, no. On holiday. From the north coast.' There was a simple friendliness about her. That wonderful mouth was still smiling at him and as she held the book against her chest he was pleasantly aware of a tantalising roundness beneath the sweater. 'I don't want to miss anything important.'

After that it was easy. Harry Benson became

Marie Gordon's guide to the delights of Sydney. For ten days they met each afternoon as soon as Harry was released from work. By ferry, bus, train, they explored the city, its parks and beaches, until, warmed by Marie Gordon's easy-going friendliness and unconscious sensuality, Harry's dormant drives readily sprang back to life.

He began to plan his moves: taking her hand as they walked, looking deep into her eyes as he wiped ice-cream from her chin, casually resting his arm across her shoulders as they sat on the ferry bench. But while Marie Gordon made no definite response to his overtures, Harry knew that what a girl didn't do was every bit as important as what she did. Marie never drew away, never shrugged him off, showed no sign of displeasure at Harry's little intimacies. Harry knew it was going to be all right.

Two days before she was due to leave he took her to the San Martino restaurant. It was the perfect setting; candles flickering romantically in encrusted bottles, soft, old-fashioned music, good food, a bottle of the patron's surreptitiously produced and ridiculously expensive wine.

They enjoyed the companionable ease that had existed between them almost from the start. Marie laughed with satisfying gusto at Harry's jokes, her eyes sparkling even more brightly after her second glass of wine.

'So, have you enjoyed your holiday?'

She turned those wide, dark eyes towards him. To Harry she looked achingly vulnerable.

'Oh, gosh yes! It's been wonderful. I was so lucky to meet you, Harry. It's made all the difference.'

Warm spurts of anticipation shooting through him, Harry reached for her hand across the table. 'I've enjoyed it too.'

It wasn't a lie. Marie's company to look forward to had made his dull working hours more bearable. There was no denying her sweetness and charm. Now he was ready to sample more physical delights.

It happened just as he planned. She accepted his suggestion of a nightcap back at his tiny, spartan apartment—spotlessly tidy, the bed freshly changed. He offered her a brandy and Marie giggled nervously as she sat on the one chair next to the bed. 'Oh, no! I thought you were just going to make coffee, Harry. I'm not really used to drinking, you know.'

Harry knew.

Five minutes later they were kissing. It was simple then to slide her off the chair and across the bed. She protested, of course, when he started to unbutton her blouse, but Harry murmured reassuringly as his feverish fingers found those wonderful breasts. Only a few minutes later her protest gave way to moans as he demonstrated his expertise with the female flesh. This was Harry's territory. Unrushed and confident, he truly delighted in giving pleasure.

The french letter was where he had left it under the pillow. He slipped it on while his tongue was busy in her mouth. As he lurched forward, burying himself inside her, he watched her face. The dark eyes widened—surely not in surprise—then shut and looked away. Harry sighed. Taking his time, ever the considerate lover, he eventually brought the act to a most satisfactory conclusion.

Only as he began to emerge from his ricochet around the universe did Harry become aware of her baffled sobs.

'Marie?' He was genuinely concerned. 'What's wrong, darling?'

'I shouldn't have done it…I didn't mean…'

He wrapped her shaking body in his arms. 'Oh, darling, there's no need to feel guilty. We both enjoyed it. And no one's being hurt.'

She didn't reply. But the tears stopped and he fell asleep in her arms.

When he woke he was alone. She was gone.

And Harry was surprised by his sharp pang of regret. For a few lazy moments he lay relishing the memory of the night before. The sweet taste of that mouth, the heavy fullness of her breasts, the perfume of her hair. He felt his erection grow and wished she were still there so they could do it all over again.

But of course, he told himself as he swung out of the musky sheets to pad naked into the mouse-hole of a bathroom, there was still the night ahead. And the next. He'd call her as soon as he got to the office.

The note was propped up against his shaving mug. Harry's smile died as he read its message.

Dear Harry,

I never meant for last night to happen and I am so terribly ashamed. You said we weren't hurting anyone else, well I guess I should have told you earlier. Only there didn't seem any point when I was there for such a short time. Derek and I have been together since we were fifteen and I love him very, very much. He's in the army at training camp in WA at the moment. But we're getting married later this year. It was how we always planned things. Now I've betrayed him and I can't begin to tell you how guilty and ashamed I feel. This is

> a secret I'm going to have to live with for the rest of my life, but I blame myself, not you. I should have seen the danger signals. Please Harry, don't try to see me again. I couldn't bear it.

Something happened inside him then. As he looked down at the words Marie Gordon had written, Harry remembered not just the warm pleasure of her body but also her innocence and vulnerability, her sense of humour, her vibrancy and enthusiasm.

Suddenly he was overcome by an emotion he had never experienced before. A piercing sense of loss. He recalled how much he had looked forward to seeing her at the end of his working day, how the warmth and sparkle in those dark eyes had invariably lifted his spirits. Marie Gordon, he realised numbly, had been special. Very special.

Struggling through the rest of the day, Harry's awareness of what Marie had come to mean to him grew achingly sharper. Half a dozen times he reached to lift the phone, dial the number of her motel. Each time, through sheer force of will, he managed to resist. It was her pain he was thinking of. To call her now would only add to her torment. And, he was forced to admit, certain rejection would hardly do much for his own state of mind.

But in the end the force of his personal torture was too great. He rang from a call box after he left the office. A sharp female voice at the other end announced that Miss Gordon had checked out, leaving no forwarding address.

With a tightness in his chest, Harry hung up. He realised then how little attention he had paid to whatever Marie might have told him about her background. Home was somewhere on the north coast. What else? Wait a moment...that was right. She was a secretary! She worked in a legal firm. He remembered now. They'd shared a joke about the stodgy dullards with whom they were forced to spend their working hours. But the name of the firm escaped him.

Harry again struggled to put her out of his mind. There was someone else, that's what she'd written. And she loved him. What hope could there be for that conniving seducer Harry Benson? I'll get over it, he told himself as the days passed. Hell, he could have his pick of dozens of girls. He didn't need to moon over Marie Gordon. He'd get *over* it.

Harry tried. Girlfriends came and went. But no one could compare with Marie. That was when he began his search. Spent hours combing the telephone directories of coastal towns, his pockets heavy with coins as he made his systematic enquiries.

Three weeks after he started he found her. Coffs Harbour. The firm of Doolan and Associates. His hand was shaking as he replaced the receiver.

That night he wrote her a letter in care of her work address, poured out his torment and love, begging her to reply. When ten days later no answer had arrived, he wrote again, his second letter a more intense appeal, if possible, than the first.

This time she wrote back. He felt his stomach turn to water as he read the brief, typed reply: 'Harry, I'm getting married. Please don't contact me again.'

The words drummed in his mind like the refrain of some funeral hymn as he laboured over his hateful rows of figures. Getting married...The one girl in the world he wanted so much.

Two weekends later, Harry could bear it no longer. He'd lost weight and had already made two serious errors at work. He knew he had to see her, try to make her understand. He'd do anything. Stick uncomplainingly with accountancy, move to the coast, turn his life upside down, anything to make her happy.

CHAPTER ONE

He borrowed a car and left early on Saturday morning. The journey took longer than he expected and he arrived in the town centre a little after noon. The local newsagent was just closing up shop.

'Gordon? Marie Gordon?' The heavily built man screwed up his face, accentuating the sun damage. 'Yeah. They're Swannson Drive, number 13.'

Harry blurted out his grateful thanks and began to hurry away when the man called after him. 'Hey, hang on, if you're one of the guests you'll find 'em down at the golf club by now.' He looked at his watch. 'You're a bit bloody late for the church.'

Harry felt his heart turn to ice. The blood evaporated in his veins. Slowly he walked back to the shopkeeper. 'Church?'

'Yeah.' The man had locked the shop door and was bending to pick up a bundle of newspapers. 'You're here for the wedding, aren't you?'

Following the newsagent's directions, Harry took less than five minutes to find the long, low brick building that was the Colony Park golf club. As he burst into the foyer, his confusion obvious, the girl behind the desk smiled and pointed down a corridor to the left.

'The wedding? Down there. Hope they've saved you some chicken.'

Harry knew he should have left then. Got back into the car and driven non-stop until he reached Sydney. But some demon compelled him and, without a word of thanks to the smiling receptionist, he hurried in the direction she had indicated.

Through the closed doors at the end of the corridor he could hear a band playing an off-key rendition of some outdated melody. Face pale and perspiring, he inched open one side of the double doors. The noise billowed out at him. But Harry barely noticed. His frantic eyes found her at once. The smiling, beautiful bride in the high-necked white gown. Being swept around the dance floor by the man whose brutal haircut confirmed him as her soldier husband.

'Lookin' for someone, mate?' A ruddy-faced guest looking too hot in his suit had poked his head around the door.

Harry shook his head.

Four months later, on yet another night when he relinquished the fight for sleep, Harry seated himself at his Laminex-topped table and began to write. He wrote the story as he had wished it might have ended. He called himself Andrew and Marie, Jan. And for the first time since his pain began, Harry found a sort of solace. With feverish dedication he lost himself in his world of words and was able to relive again and again that short, intense time of joy.

Those pages, written in the sullen hours of night, set him on the path to international success. *From the Heart* was the story Harry was driven to tell. And in the novels that followed he tapped his suffering to tell the stories that touched the hearts of millions of women throughout the world. Yet the only heart he had wanted for his own he could never have.

But now...He picked up the receiver and heard her voice and for a moment was unable to force a sound from his own throat. Finally—'Nice to catch up...Are you free? Dinner?' Somehow he managed to achieve coherency.

'That sounds nice, Harry. I've followed your career with interest. Read all your books, you know.'

Light laugh. Harry Benson, celebrity. 'Great. So have I. That'll give us something to talk about.'

He took her somewhere so dimly lit and out-of-the-way that no one would be likely to recognise or bother him. Nothing must distract him. It was an evening Harry had dreamed of so often, had imagined in endless permutations in his books without ever imagining it could possibly come true. But here he was. Sitting across from her, looking into those same dark eyes, lined now, but still as vulnerable and enchanting as in her youth.

'You've forgiven me?' It was the question he had to ask and he had left it until the end. Up till then they had caught up on the less dangerous threads in the tapestry of their lives. She had one daughter, Michelle, married, living in London. Marie herself managed a small homewares store in Chatswood Place. She had moved to Sydney after her husband's death. Cancer. But he'd gone quickly, thank God.

Not quickly enough for Harry.

She was smiling at him now as he waited for her to answer his question.

'It was myself I found hard to forgive, Harry. In the end I managed to forgive the deed. What was harder to deal with was the fact that I couldn't quite forget you.' She looked away, but spoke with the same directness that had delighted him all those years ago.

Harry wondered if she could hear the sonic boom of his heart. 'I never forgot you, Marie. No one ever took your place.'

She raised her head. Their eyes met and Harry reached across the table and folded her hand in his own.

The women's magazines couldn't get enough of

CHAPTER ONE

'Harry Benson's True-Life Love Story.' The news broke three days after Harry and Marie were married in the garden of his rambling stone villa near St Paul-de-Vence.

The ceremony, attended by a select few, included Marie's surprised and delighted daughter, Michelle, who flew in from London. As might be expected, true love, vintage champagne and a spectacular setting made for a glorious occasion. If Harry had the tiniest regret it was that Eleanor Martin had not lived to be present. She would, he felt sure, have been delighted to meet the source of his inspiration.

Later, safely on their honeymoon by the lakes of northern Italy, Harry was only too pleased to allow his publicists to announce his joy to the world.

Around the globe millions of his adoring female fans experienced a myriad of emotions as they pored over the wedding photographs and the—somewhat edited—story of Harry Benson's lost love. Side by side with nostalgia for a happy ending to the real-life story of their favourite author there was also regret and, it must be admitted, some unsheathed jealousy for the woman who Harry Benson so openly admitted was his creative inspiration. Sharp eyes from Madrid to Minnesota raked over Mrs Harry

Benson's hairstyle, her spring-flower headdress and cream antique lace suit.

But his fans were the last thing on Harry's mind as he cradled his wife beneath the billowing net of the four-poster bed in Bellagio's Grand Hotel. Love oozed from every pore of his body. He could hardly bear to let her out of his sight for a moment.

'I can't believe it. I just can't believe it.' It was a refrain he found himself repeating as he and Marie took breakfast on their balcony overlooking the lake, as they strolled around the steep, winding streets, as they sat with their Camparis on the terrace before dinner. 'It's a dream come true, darling,' he whispered as his new wife smiled and squeezed his hand.

Harry's joy in his marriage, in his reunion with the woman to whom his heart had always belonged, made him brim with new energy and zest. They had barely settled back into their Sydney home when he was planning their next trip, eager to share the fruits of his success with the woman who had so amazingly re-entered his life.

For Marie, while poised and self-assured, had led a sheltered existence. After a series of army postings her husband's return to civilian life had taken them back to the town where they'd both grown up. Life as the wife of a small-town hardware store manager could not have offered much opportunity for excitement.

Harry was determined to show his love the world. They seemed to spend months in the air, alighting in New York or Barbados, Antigua or Kentucky, Gstaad or Verona. Harry spoilt his wife in five-star hotels, with couturier gowns and spectacular jewellery, all the while ignoring her gentle protests at the abundance of his generosity.

'Harry, it's not necessary. I'm not used to all this.' They were sitting in the private salon of Chaumet, the oldest and most distinguished jewellers in France, a sea of emeralds sparkling on velvet pads before them.

'Darling,' Harry stroked her cheek, 'it's been six months. This is to mark the occasion.'

With the media interest as keen as ever, Harry would often insist that Marie be included in the interviews. He overrode her protestations. 'Don't be silly, darling. The world should hear our story, see us together. Just think of the hope we can bring others dreaming of a happy ending.'

Thankfully, however, by the time their first anniversary approached, life had become more settled. Even Harry began to appreciate the simple pleasures of spending time together at home. They would read, sit in the garden, occasionally entertain, visit the opera or theatre. An idyllic existence.

It was Marie who raised the subject first. 'Darling, have you started thinking about a new book?'

Harry smiled at her over the dinner table. 'Authors are always thinking about their work, my sweet.'

'When do you think you might start on this one?'

'Any day now. Any day.' His green eyes twinkled. 'We've had a bit on our plate for a while, you must admit.'

The telephone call from his publishers a week later put basically the same question. Publishers like profits. And Harry Benson was profit incarnate. Also, they reminded him encouragingly, he had his public to think of. It had been almost eighteen months. His fans were hungry for another heart-wrenching tale by Harry Benson. And of course with all the publicity about his marriage...well, the time was ripe, wasn't it?

It was the prod Harry needed. The very next day he fell back into the routine he'd followed over nearly 30 years. Half an hour after breakfast he kissed his wife fondly and retired to his study. There, enfolded in the familiar book-lined womb, he switched on his computer and faced the blank screen.

By lunchtime he had achieved nothing. It was a rare setback. But Harry knew he was paying the price for the disruption to his routine. Discipline. That's what writing took. Just a matter of sitting there until creativity began to flower.

By the end of the week Harry wasn't entering his study with quite the same determination as before. By the end of the second week he didn't go in at all.

'I'm exhausted. I didn't realise just how much until I took that time to be with you, my darling.' He offered his excuse to his wife's anxious face. 'In a month or so I'll give it another go.'

The month ended and Harry returned to his task. It was no easier than before. As he deleted idea after idea from the accusing screen, he felt the beginnings of panic. What was happening to him? Why wasn't it working?

He didn't need the money, but he *had to write.* It was all he knew. It was what made him Harry Benson.

The problem began to take its toll. He avoided going into the room where his creative juices had soured. He lied to his agent and his publishers when they caught him by phone. He turned down interviews with the press and an invitation to open a writers' festival in Mexico City.

But he couldn't hide his emotional state from his wife.

'Harry, the only thing that's changed is having me around. Maybe it's that.' A worried Marie forced him to address the problem one night after dinner. 'I've read that writers need solitude, lots of time alone. You've never had to write with someone around 24 hours a day. You need to be on your own for a while, darling. Why don't I visit Michelle in London? That'd give you the space you need.'

Harry's eyes widened in panic. 'But I'll miss you so much! Honestly, darling, it's not *you*! It's *me*. It's just a matter of finding the right story, that's all.'

In the end she managed to persuade him. After all, he had to accept the fact that she was a mother too.

'Just three weeks, my love. That's all you'll need to get started again, I'll bet. You'll be able to concentrate only on your work, get back into your proper routine.'

'I'll miss you.'

Marie smiled at his rueful expression. 'And of course I'll miss you, my darling. But think how lovely it'll be when we see each other again.'

CHAPTER ONE

Each day seemed like a millennium. She rang three times a week and Harry lived for her calls.

'How's it going? The cold snap not getting you down?'

Her laugh reached him down the line. 'Typical London, isn't it? At this time of year! No, we're off to the theatre tomorrow night. Some drama the critics are raving about.'

'Well, give Michelle my love. I miss you darling, very much. Goodbye. Love you.'

'And I love you too, my sweet.'

She knew better than to ask how he was going. And Harry would have hated it if she had. Because nothing had changed. Each day his sense of panic grew stronger. Each attempt at a story ended in frustration and despair. Idea after idea faded into nothing.

And now, in 72 hours, she would be home. What would it matter then that another fruitless day lay behind him? For Harry had come to a decision. His writing days were behind him. The compulsion was gone. And what did it matter? Money would never be a problem. No, he had accepted the fact that the time had come to retire. From now on his time and energy would be reserved for the woman he loved to the very core of his being.

He was getting ready to retire to his unbearably lonely bed when the telephone's ring broke the silence. London! It must be. His spirits soaring, he snatched up the receiver. At the other end of the line the voice was clear and distinct but for a long, static moment the words didn't make any sense.

'What...what are you telling me?'

The words drowned him again and he dropped onto the bed. A paralysis crept over him, shackling his entire body. 'Yes...yes...thank you for letting me know.' Good manners, even now. He stuttered a goodnight to her daughter's husband and slowly replaced the receiver. Impaled on his numbness, he did not move and hardly breathed.

Some time later, foetus-like, he curled up on the bed and trumpeted his grief.

For a long time he locked himself away. Refused to see anyone. The press were the worst. He released a statement through his publicists, but it wasn't enough. The media invariably want more. But what more could be said? An icy road, treacherous conditions. Two vehicles slewing into the post-theatre crowds.

With his writer's imagination he drew the scene again and again. Steamy breath in the night air, those dark laughing eyes turned towards her daughter. Then screams. And arterial blood spurting onto her bright yellow coat and the grey, hard pavement where she died. Later, he went away. Spent the northern spring in a spartan hotel on some island off Greece. Where nobody knew him. Where he could sit and think. Walk and think. Sleep and not think. With a little help.

And then he went home. To see the blooms on the bushes she had planted. To run his fingers over the curtains she had chosen. To sit in the sofa where she had rested and laughed.

Not long afterwards he went into his study and the words came easily.

Readers of popular fiction are looking for a story that intrigues and entertains, so to catch their interest you must start with a bang. The short story form is no exception.

The Gift arose out of my musings on the motivations behind creativity. I liked the irony in the scenario of a writer who loses the hunger to write after he is reunited with the source of his creativity, the woman who makes his life happy and complete. The slightly overblown writing style seemed to suit the ironic edge.

In *The Gift* I begin by introducing Harry Benson as a success and describing the extent of his riches. What I don't do is tell my readers immediately how he amassed such wealth. For all they know at the opening of the story, Harry might be a drug dealer, a corrupt businessman or a world-famous composer. A common error of beginner writers is to tell too much too quickly. Never forget that suspense and intrigue are heightened if you delay answering the questions you set up for your readers.

Yet for all that, a short story must obviously tell a tale as concisely as possible, and I waste no time in filling in Harry's background—insofar as it has direct relevance to the story. All my readers need to know here is that Harry started out as a shy country boy who was encouraged in his studies by a teacher. I give Mrs Daley no more than a mention as Harry's mentor. Nor do I describe Harry's mother—though I imply that their relationship is a good one by saying she was proud of his academic success and sad when he left for Sydney.

The first turning point in this story comes when Harry finds that his intense dislike of his academic course is matched only by his attraction to the opposite sex. The fact that Harry connects so well with women makes credible his ability to relate to them in his writing. And it is at this point that I reveal that it's through his novels that Harry has become such a success. To maintain the intrigue, I then refer to 'someone' who has been the catalyst for this brilliant career. But rather than go into detail here, I flash back to trace the path of Harry's progress.

At this point I introduce the secondary character Eleanor Martin. There is no need to describe her in detail beyond a brief mention of her age. Her role is to provide the momentum that launches Harry's writing career. To show how enormously successful this is, I tell of the international hits, the film deals and Harry's continuing appeal for his female fans despite the passage of years.

I return readers to the present with this intriguing sentence: 'Life might have continued on this quite acceptable path if not for what occurred one April morning in the year Harry turned 51.' This introduces the second turning point when Harry accidentally bumps into Marie. I show her effect on Harry as he waits for her to call—and this gives me the perfect opportunity to fill in more details about Harry who, despite his wealth and success, is fearful of real intimacy with a woman, and also sketch in important parts of the back-plot: how he and Marie met, and parted, and his anguished search for her.

Now I have told my readers all they need to know to appreciate the intensity of the renewed relationship between these two middle-aged lovers. A marriage is inevitable, of course, and at this point in the story readers will be expecting a happy ending.

But, breaking one of the rules of popular-fiction writing, I avoid this.

I now introduce the idea of how love can overpower an artist's creative 'hunger'. Harry gives not a moment's thought to his work as he spends the first six months of his marriage in almost perpetual motion, showing his lost love the world. The next turning point comes when Marie brings up the question of when he is going to start writing again.

Tracing Harry's struggles and finally his relieved decision to give up his career for love makes the tragedy of Marie's death all the more agonising—and lends a sombre touch to the ending, as Harry's second loss ironically restores his creative gift.

See how much can be achieved in such a short tale. Flashbacks, intrigue, intense emotion. You may find it a useful and interesting exercise to try writing the story from Marie's point of view. Areas and issues to explore might include: her family background, her reaction to her meeting with Harry, how she felt on her first wedding day, her attitude to her husband and marriage, how she felt when her husband died, her reaction to bumping into Harry again...Try it, and see how much intrigue and emotion you can bring to your own telling of the story of these two star-crossed lovers.

Over to you

Well, there it is. I hope that working through this book has left you feeling more confident and better equipped to develop your own storylines.

Perhaps they'll be ones stimulated by the beginnings on offer here, maybe they'll be ones you've had in the back of your mind for years. Whatever the case, you'll never know if you have talent or not if you don't sit down and begin the manuscript you're dreaming about.

It isn't easy, as you will know from having read about my own struggles with beginings. It takes discipline and sacrifice. All I can do at this point therefore is to reiterate my closing statements in *Creating Popular Fiction:*

- Don't procrastinate a moment longer.
- Start that novel today—and don't let *anything* stop you finishing it.
- The best of luck!

Epilogue
Getting it finished

THIS book has provided you with a collection of intriguing beginnings, one of which might excite your imagination enough to get you finally started on writing that novel.

You may use any of the beginning chapters in Part 2 without fear of breaching copyright. But even if you don't actually borrow any of these chapter openings, you should still find them and the analyses a source of invaluable information about how to create your own original story.

Don't forget, though, that ideas, plots, storylines, do not magically write themselves. Now you need the discipline to sit down and begin. In *Creating Popular Fiction* I explain how to establish a routine with your writing. Even if you only write a page a day, it's important to keep doing so until it becomes a habit like cleaning your teeth. That's the only way you're ever going to complete that novel you've been dreaming of. And to see the finished manuscript will, I promise, bring you enormous satisfaction.

Will it be published?

You'll never know unless you start.